RAMEN

JAPANESE NOODLES *and* SIDE DISHES

ラーメン TOVE NILSSON

PAVILION

001

WAIT / CHOOSE / SLURP

The best ramen places often have a long queue outside. Pictured here is Tokyo Ramen Street, a collection of ramen restaurants underneath Tokyo station.

CONTENTS

食 券

店長イチオシ! 醤油味　魚介系のあっさり! 塩味　日本初!ココでしか食べられない ベジソバ

① 特製江戸式中華そば 1,100 yen
④ 味玉中華そば 920 yen
⑪ [限定80食] 特製角煮塩ラーメン 1,200 yen
⑥ 特製ベジソバ 1,100 yen

⑤ ゆず中華そば 920 yen
③ 江戸式中華そば 800 yen
⑫ [限定80食] 味玉塩ラーメン 1,070 yen
⑩ 玄米麺ベジソバ 1,050 yen

玄米麺の大盛りは出来ません

⑦ 「辛」中華そば 920 yen
⑯ 大盛り 120 yen
⑮ 半熟味付玉子 120 yen
⑰ ビーガン豆乳ソフトクリーム 350 yen
⑬ [限定80食] 沖縄式角煮塩ラーメン 950 yen
売切
⑦ 味玉ベジソバ 1,020 yen
⑧ ベジソバ 900 yen

⑭ ソラのスムージー 150 yen
⑲ 食べる野菜 150 yen
㉛ 角煮しぐれ煮丼 200 yen
㉑ 角煮しぐれ煮丼 350 yen
㉒ ご飯 120 yen

玄米麺は1日50食限定です

㉓ 人参100%ジュース(小) 200 yen
㉔ 人参100%ジュース(風) 400 yen
⑳ ソラの日の丸おむすび 250 yen
㉕ COEDO 600 yen
ハイボール 400 yen

カードをふれてください Suica

角煮玄米麺に変更 150 yen
㉗ お土産玄米麺1玉 250 yen
㉘ オリジナルTシャツ 3,000 yen
㉙ おつまみ角煮 500 yen
㉚ ビーガン担々麺 900 yen

1000 2000 5000 10000
紙幣

発売中

硬貨 500 100 50 10　とりけし　おつり硬貨

券（チケット）

⚠注意
取出口より奥へ手を入れないでください。

⚠警告
転倒事故を防ぐために上に乗らない揺さぶらない傾けないようにしてください。

002
WAIT / CHOOSE / SLURP

If you're worried about things getting lost in translation, most ramen places have a vending machine right inside the restaurant doors where you can easily choose your food.

003

WAIT / CHOOSE / SLURP

You won't have to wait for long before a hot bowl with noodles is placed in front of you. Now you just have to start slurping. Pictured here is tonkotsu ramen at Ippudo in Ebisu, Tokyo.

FOREWORD

I AM A RAMEN ADDICT. Every time I've travelled abroad over the past ten years I've looked for ramen joints. What has struck me while queueing outside the best ramen bars is that it seems there are a lot of people just like me who are always on the hunt for their next fix.

It all starts with a large bowl filled to the brim with steaming hot broth that's been simmering for up to 48 hours. The flavour has been boosted with dried mushrooms, seaweed, miso and dried fish, and the broth's perfect surface is covered in small droplets of fat. Thin, springy noodles are folded into the deep bowl and topped with chashu pork belly, a soy marinated egg and many other delicious things.

Few dishes are so addictive, and you can be served the simplest to the most complex flavour combinations at the shabbiest joints in Tokyo and the hottest places in LA.

Until a year or so ago, ramen wasn't very common in my native Sweden, either in home kitchens or in the restaurant world – with the exception of the small packets of instant noodles that arrived in the 90s. I fell for them too, of course, and cooked them up with extra spices and vegetables, but it wasn't until I started eating genuine ramen that I realised how it should really taste.

When I couldn't find good ramen locally I started cooking it at home. I experimented in the kitchen to develop the best noodles and boiled broth for hours to get the ultimate flavour. When visiting ramen bars, I sat and observed how the chefs worked, what the broth looked like, how long they boiled the noodles for, how many bowls of tare (flavourings) they had, which kind of eggs they served and how well marinated their chashu pork was.

All the knowledge I've gathered together in this book will hopefully provide a greater understanding of how a dish as simple as noodles in broth can give so much satisfaction and sensational flavour.

1.

2.

3.

4.

5.

6.

TOOLS

There are several specialist cooking tools that will make life easier when it comes to preparing ramen. Of course, you can manage most things with a knife, a saucepan and a frying pan, but it all flows more efficiently and feels more enjoyable when you have the right tools to hand. You'll find the following in Asian shops or online. Some items you might pick up when you travel overseas – the authentic stuff you buy abroad is always the most fun to use!

1. PASTA MACHINE

The easiest way to make noodles is to use a pasta or noodle machine. I've got a pasta attachment for my KitchenAid, which means I don't have to turn it by hand, but a manual one works well too. You can find Japanese noodle machines online, from simpler plastic ones to pretty expensive ones that knead, roll and cut. If you haven't got a machine, you can of course roll, fold and cut the dough by hand, just like you do with udon and soba.

2. RAMEN LADLE

Good to slurp broth with and to catch the drips underneath the noodles when you eat. A standard tablespoon will work too, of course, or you can drink the broth straight from the bowl.

3. KATSUOBUSHI GRATER BOX

If you're lucky enough to find a whole katsuobushi block (dried whole tuna) you should also have a specialist grater, as the fish is extremely hard and difficult to grate in any other way. The box is, however, hard to get hold of in the West, and you often have to make do with bags of the ready-grated stuff.

4. BLOWTORCH

To get an extra tasty surface on chashu pork and other meat you can use a blowtorch. Many ramen joints use this technique: you can colour the meat quickly and heat thin slices up without having to use the oven.

5. SESAME MILL

The best invention. I always used to crush my sesame seeds with a pestle and mortar to get more flavour out of them, but with a sesame mill you can grind them straight over the noodle bowl. The difference between ground and whole sesame seeds is extreme. Try it: you will never want to eat whole seeds again!

6. NOODLE STRAINER

If you haven't got a noodle basket, a noodle strainer is the next best thing; perfect especially for udon and soba noodles. You cook the noodles directly in the water and remove them using the large strainer.

7. MANDOLIN

Thinly sliced vegetables like daikon, ginger and onion are best if you slice them on a mandolin. Place the sliced vegetables in ice-cold water for extra crunchiness.

8. NOODLE BASKET

The best way to cook noodles is to use a noodle basket. You stick 2–4 baskets into a pan with water on a rolling boil. Each noodle portion is cooked separately, drained thoroughly and then goes straight into the bowl with the broth. Since they are quite rich in starch, the noodles can stick together in the colander if you cook and drain them all together. To ensure that the noodles don't stick together while cooking, stir with chopsticks until they separate.

9. ROLLING PIN

A small Asian rolling pin is good for rolling udon and soba dough. A smaller rolling pin means that it's easier to use your own body weight to work the firm dough.

10. LADLE

You need a proper soup ladle for ladling the broth into serving bowls.

11. OKONOMIYAKI COVER

To make the perfect okonomiyaki you should fry it covered with a lid so that the cabbage softens. You can buy special okonomiyaki covers in Japan, but for the home kitchen you can also use aluminium foil or a standard lid.

12. KNIFE

When cutting your noodles, you will need a knife with a flat edge, such as a cleaver, so that you get an even cut in the dough. I buy my noodle knives in Asian shops. There are also specialist udon and soba knives.

13. CHOPSTICKS

The obvious choice for eating ramen and also useful as a stirring tool when cooking the noodles.

INGREDIENTS

Most ingredients needed for ramen can be found in large supermarkets these days, but do venture into an Asian shop if you're lucky enough to live near one. Specialist Japanese ingredients can be particularly difficult to find, for example dried bonito (katsuobushi), Japanese mayonnaise and okonomiyaki sauce. You can also find many of the following products online.

1. WHITE AND RED MISO PASTE

There are a handful of different kinds of miso; I mostly use white and red. The white is slightly milder and sweeter, whereas the red has a bit more of a punch. They can be combined to make a nice blend.

2. KATSUOBUSHI

A rock-hard block of dried, smoked tuna that requires a special grater. Katsuobushi is a umami bomb and adds a deep, slightly smoky flavour to the broth.

3. CORIANDER

If you can, buy fresh coriander from Asian food shops because they sell it with the root still attached. The root is also tasty chopped up and added to spice pastes and broths, or finely shredded as a topping.

4. SHRIMP PASTE

Add for a umami kick and 'funky' fish flavour.

5. SESAME OIL

Use toasted sesame oil; untoasted is not the same thing at all.

6. BEAN AND CHILLI PASTE

Fermented Chinese bean and chilli paste. It is usually made with broad beans or soya beans.

7. BONITO FLAKES

Grated thin flakes of katsuobushi (dried smoked tuna) that are used as a topping for ramen and okonomiyaki, or for mixing together with salt.

8. JAPANESE SOY SAUCE

A lighter soy sauce than the Chinese version, with a fantastic saltiness and umami flavour.

9. CHINESE SOY SAUCE

Darker soy sauce made from mushrooms, with slightly burnt notes in its intense salty flavour.

10. KEWPIE MAYO

Japanese mayonnaise with slightly more acidity than what you might be used to. Nothing beats it drizzled over an okonomiyaki or a sushi roll.

11. YUZU

A fruit with the taste and smell of lemon mixed with fragrant mandarin. Fresh yuzu has a short season, so make sure you use both the zest and the juice if you can get hold of one. You can also buy packaged yuzu juice that actually isn't too bad for using in ponzu dressing and for flavouring broths.

12. SEAWEED

The seaweeds I use the most are kombu, wakame and nori. Kombu is added when cooking broth to give extra umami flavour; wakame is nice served in broths and soups; while nori can be served in broth or used as a topping for okonomiyaki, udon noodles and tsukemen noodles. It can also be blended together with salt.

13. SHICHIMI TOGARASHI

Japanese spice mix made with Sichuan pepper, chilli and sesame seeds, among other things.

14. MIRIN

A sweet rice wine that traditionally gets its sweetness from fermentation, without adding any sugar. Unfortunately it's difficult to find this type of 'genuine' mirin in the West, so we often have to make do with a sweetened vinegar.

15. OKONOMIYAKI SAUCE

This sauce is a must for okonomiyaki. If you can't get hold of any, you can make your own (see page 139).

16. SAKE

This is a Japanese rice brew and not a spirit, as many people believe. The alcohol content is never more than 20 percent and the method of production is actually more similar to brewing beer than distilling spirits.

17. SESAME SEEDS

There are both black and white sesame seeds. They get their nutty and tasty character from being toasted. They should ideally be ground or crushed using a pestle and mortar or sesame mill after being toasted, to bring out the best flavour and aroma.

18. KOREAN DRIED CHILLI

If you are looking for dried chilli that you can use a lot of without choking on the heat, the Korean chilli (gochugaru) is a good choice. It has a flavour of bell peppers and gives a nice red colour to chilli oil, spice pastes and dipping sauces.

19. POTATO FLOUR

To achieve the perfect starchy noodles, I use potato flour or cornflour.

20. DRIED SHIITAKE

Shiitake, black morels or black fungus are the dried mushrooms that I think work best for ramen. They add flavour to broths and they can also be pickled or used as a topping.

21. KOREAN CHILLI PASTE

Fermented Korean chilli paste (gochujang) is a staple that belongs in every fridge. Just the right heat, a nice delicate sweetness and a lot of flavour. It's used, among other things, as a tare (flavouring) for kimchi ramen (see page 58).

001
BASICS

Ramen is actually a pretty simple food. Good noodles, broth and toppings. But as with everything else that seems simple, attention to detail is key. The wheat noodles should have the right springiness and thickness, the broth should be aromatic and have depth and a bit of punch, and the topping should be simple but well executed. Pictured here is a selection of ramen baskets for sale and traditional Japanese dishes served at the large catering store Kappabashi in north Tokyo.

BROTH

THE BROTH IS INCREDIBLY IMPORTANT IN A RAMEN. More important than the actual noodles. You can buy perfectly decent noodles in a shop, but finding a broth that beats one slowly simmered away at home is impossible.

We can divide Japanese ramen broths into three different basic types. The first is a pure chicken broth that's used for shio and shoyu ramen. It has a very clean taste and is made from just water and really good-quality chicken. The second is a broth made from both chicken and pork, where the flavours have been enhanced by adding dried mushroom, seaweed, miso and dried tuna to get a broth as deep and flavourful as possible. The last variety is the renowned tonkotsu: a broth cooked for up to 48 hours made from just pork and water, sometimes with a little onion added. The broth ends up milky white and thick from all the fat and collagen in the trotters and shanks. There are also broths made from fish and seafood but they are not as common.

All the broths fall into two categories: kotteri, a rich broth with lots of flavour and texture; and assari, a lighter broth that is often quite clear and transparent. I love a thick kotteri broth with a base of tonkotsu that's been flavoured with sesame and chilli.

At the time of cooking the broth, you don't season at all. Salt is only added when serving, and the amount depends on what the broth is flavoured with. All broths can be served as they are with just a pinch of salt, but they are usually flavoured with a tare (flavouring). A tare can be soy sauce, a spice paste or an oil. The exception is mushroom broth, which I usually add soy sauce and salt to just after cooking. It needs a bit of saltiness to not feel flat since it doesn't contain any fat or other flavour carriers, unlike the meat broths.

Many chefs, both in Japan and elsewhere, create their own ramen broths to put their unique stamp on the flavour. One example is the chef David Chang. At his renowned New York restaurant, Momofuku, they serve a ramen made from broth that has been boiled with everything you can imagine: beef, bone marrow, pork trotters, pork shanks, root vegetables, onion, smoky bacon, kombu, shiitake. The result is a broth extremely complex in flavour and some Japanese would probably feel a little uncomfortable if they knew the insane ingredient list. But at the same time, it's the result that counts, and it is incredibly slurp-friendly.

The main thing is to forget everything you've learnt about making broth and stock from the classic French kitchen. Stocks and broths that are simmered gently until you get a clear and almost transparent colour are, according to the Japanese, absolutely bonkers. Sieving the broth through muslin for a clear consommé also goes against all ramen thinking. You're after all those bits that have broken away from the bones, meat and vegetables during cooking – all of which are nutrients that make the broth healthy and delicious.

Many ramen broths, like tonkotsu, should boil and steam heavily to get the maximum amount of flavour and nutrients, while chicken broth should be cooked at a slightly lower heat.

The secret behind a delicious broth is a long cooking time and quality ingredients.

DASHI

Despite its short ingredients list and zero cooking time, dashi has a deep, complex and slightly smoky flavour. The components are jam-packed with the magic taste, umami, that the Japanese are masters of: dried seaweed, dried smoked tuna and dried mushroom. You can mix dashi with another broth such as miso to use as a tare. When serving the dashi warm with noodles, udon and soba are the most popular choices. You can also mix dashi with soy sauce, grated daikon and spring onion to make a dipping sauce for soba noodles.

MAKES APPROXIMATELY 2 LITRES/
3 ½ PINTS/8 CUPS

2 litres/3½ pints/8 cups cold water

10 pieces of kombu seaweed (30g/1oz)

20g/¾oz/1¾ cups bonito flakes

10 dried shiitake mushrooms (15g/½oz)

30g/1oz/scant ¼ cup dried white fish, optional

salt

1. Mix all the ingredients together in a large bowl. Cover with clingfilm or a lid. Leave to stand for 3–12 hours at room temperature. The longer you leave it the more intense flavour you will get. If it stands for 12 hours you might even have to dilute it with more water. But if you're in a rush and need an emergency dashi, 3 hours will be enough.

2. When you are ready to serve, heat up the liquid to approximately 80°C/176°F. Don't let it boil or some of the aromas and flavours will be ruined.

3. Remove from the heat and leave to stand for 5 minutes.

4. Before serving, the broth can be salted and flavoured with tare (flavouring) of your choice.

PORK AND CHICKEN BROTH

This is a mixed broth made with both chicken and pork. It is incredibly delicious as you get a more complex flavour which is boosted by the dried mushrooms, seaweed, ginger and dried smoked tuna. You can throw in a little bit of what you fancy or what you happen to have at home. Many people make a broth from pork belly and some root vegetables. I tend to be a bit cautious with the root vegetables though, because they can give the broth a sweet flavour that isn't too pleasant after a few spoonfuls.

MAKES APPROXIMATELY 2½–3 LITRES/
4½–5¼ PINTS/10½–14¼ CUPS

4 litres/7 pints/16 cups water

1 chicken carcass or 2 chicken thighs

400g/14oz pork belly

2 pieces of kombu seaweed (6g/⅛oz)

6 dried shiitake mushrooms (10g/¼oz)

10cm/4in ginger root, sliced

4 whole spring onions

4 tbsp bonito flakes (katsuobushi)

salt

1. Place all the ingredients apart from the bonito flakes and salt in a pan that holds approximately 6 litres/10½ pints/25 cups.

2. Bring to the boil and skim off the foam once it has started boiling.

3. Add the bonito flakes and leave to simmer uncovered for 3–5 hours.

4. Strain and save the broth. The pork belly can be used as a ramen topping.

5. Before serving, the broth can be salted and flavoured with tare (flavouring) of your choice.

CHICKEN BROTH

It might seem a bit odd to make a broth from only chicken and water when you're used to the classic recipes with celery, carrot, bay leaf, parsley and onion, but here it's about total simplicity. You want a broth that tastes purely of chicken and that has been boiled for a long time to allow the fat from the skin and meat to melt into the liquid. The most important thing is to choose the best quality organic chicken for superior fat and flavour. When the broth is done it may seem bland, but once it meets salt, soy sauce, spice paste or other tare in the bowl with the noodles, you understand how a really good broth should taste. Many ramen chefs work with double broths, where they mix two types of broth to get an even more complex flavour. The most common combinations are dashi/chicken and tonkotsu/chicken.

MAKES APPROXIMATELY 5 LITRES / 8¾ PINTS / 20¾ CUPS

  1 whole chicken (approximately 1.5kg/3lb 2oz)
  5 litres/8¾ pints/20¾ cups water
  salt

1. Place the whole chicken in a large pan that holds 6 litres.

2. Add the water and bring to the boil on a low heat. Skim off the foam. Simmer for approximately 5–6 hours covered with a lid.

3. Remove the chicken and save for a topping or another recipe. Strain the broth and store in the fridge.

4. Before serving, the broth can be salted and flavoured with tare (flavouring) of your choice.

TONKOTSU BROTH

The ingredients here are simple and few. The pig's trotters contain everything you need: rind, fat, collagen and bones. You will get the best result by roasting some of the trotters before they're boiled, so that the rind turns golden brown. If you're lacking large pans or don't need a large quantity of broth, you can halve this recipe.

MAKES APPROXIMATELY 8 LITRES / 14 PINTS / 33⅓ CUPS

  15 pig's trotters, halved lengthways
  12 litres/21 pints/50 cups water
  4 onions, halved
  salt

1. Rinse the pig's trotters and place in a bowl or container. Cover with cold water. Cover with clingfilm and place in the fridge for approximately 12 hours. Change the water once if you can.

2. Drain the trotters and rinse in cold water.

3. Preheat the oven to 250°C/500°F/Gas 9.

4. Pat dry and place 12 of the halved trotters onto a baking tray. Roast in the middle of the oven for approximately 30 minutes.

5. Place the rest of the trotters and the onions in a large pan that holds approximately 20 litres. Pour over 12 litres/21 pints/50 cups of water and bring to the boil.

6. Add the roasted trotters to the pan. The broth should not simmer but boil steadily with proper bubbles, to release all the gelatine and fat. Normally about a third of the water will evaporate. If you lose too much liquid, add more water.

7. Strain the broth while it's still warm.

8. Season with salt or other tare (flavouring) just before serving.

BEEF BONE BROTH

Before I tried this beef broth at Matador Ramen in Tokyo I thought that my absolute favourite broth was tonkotsu, but now I can't make my mind up between the two! When cooking broth from beef the flavour comes from a nice fatty cut, which gives it a rich base. I use oxtail, but if unavailable I ask for beef or veal shank. I also throw in roasted marrow bones which slowly melt in the heat. Don't exclude anything here. If you cook the broth using only meat, it won't be as fatty as it should be.

MAKES APPROXIMATELY 4 LITRES/
7 PINTS/16 CUPS

> 1kg/2lb 4oz oxtail or veal shank
> 20cm/8in marrow bone
> 4.5 litres/7 pints/18¾ cups water
> 2 onions
> salt

1. Preheat the oven to 220°C/425°F/Gas 7.
2. Roast the meat and the marrow bone in the middle of the oven for approximately 30 minutes.
3. Bring the water to the boil in a large pan together with the onions.
4. Remove the tray from the oven and transfer the meat to the pan.
5. Add a cup of water to the hot tray and whisk to scrape up all the good flavours.
6. Add the roasted marrow bone to the pan together with the liquid and bits from the tray.
7. Bring to the boil and leave to simmer gently for about 6 hours covered with a lid.
8. Strain and season with salt and tare (flavouring) of your choice before serving. The oxtail meat can be picked and used as a topping.

MUSHROOM BROTH

This is a so-called assari broth, light and often translucent. Mushroom broth is sometimes served far too sweet and some regard it as watery and without flavour. It is an art to get it right. I mix together both fresh and dried mushrooms: my secret ingredient is black morels, which give even more depth and smokiness. The broth is actually only brought to the boil once and is then left to infuse away from the heat – almost like a dashi broth. Don't throw away the mushrooms that get left over from the cooking – they can be pickled together with soy sauce and rice vinegar (see recipe on page 145).

MAKES APPROXIMATELY 2 LITRES/
3½ PINTS/8 CUPS

> 12 dried shiitake mushrooms (20g/¾oz)
> 6 dried black morels
> 300g/10½oz fresh shiitake mushrooms
> 3 pieces of kombu seaweed (10g/¼oz)
> 2 spring onions
> 10cm/4in piece of ginger root, sliced
> 2.5 litres/4⅓ pints/10½ cups water
> 150ml/5fl oz/scant ⅔ cup Japanese soy sauce
> salt

1. Place the mushrooms, kombu, spring onions, ginger and water in a large pan and bring to the boil. Leave to simmer for about 30 minutes.
2. Turn off the heat and leave the broth to infuse for about 3 hours.
3. Strain the broth. Save the mushrooms for pickles.
4. To serve, heat up the broth and season with soy sauce and salt.

KOTTERI VEGGIE BROTH

A broth should be rich, with a deep umami flavour and fat that lifts up all the flavours and spices – not easy to achieve in a vegetable broth, where there's no animal fat. I wanted to make a fairly thick vegetable broth, similar to a tonkotsu or a tantanmen. What complicates things is that vegetables often have a sweet flavour, so you have to balance that with salt, acidity and fat. Salt and acidity are relatively easy; it's the fat that is the hard part. The answer is coconut oil with a neutral flavour, which acts a bit like chicken or pork fat. To get maximum flavour, the butternut squash, mushrooms and onions are first roasted with smoked paprika – I use this as a replacement for the slightly smoky bonito (dried tuna).

MAKES APPROXIMATELY 2.5 LITRES/
4 1/3 PINTS/10 1/2 CUPS

2 litres/3½ pints/8 cups water

6 dried shiitake mushrooms (10g/¼oz)

2 pieces of kombu seaweed (6g)

300g/10½oz butternut squash, diced

2 onions, cut into wedges

100g/3½oz oyster mushrooms or fresh
shiitake mushrooms

3 garlic cloves

2½ tbsp vegetable oil

2 tsp Spanish smoked paprika

2 tbsp coarsely chopped ginger root

75ml/5 tbsp Japanese soy sauce

4 tbsp white miso paste

3 tbsp rice vinegar

4 tbsp coconut oil

2 tsp salt

1. Preheat the oven to 250°C/500°F/Gas 9.

2. In a pan that holds about 3 litres/5½ pints/13¼ cups, bring the water to the boil with the shiitake and kombu. Lower the heat and simmer for 1 hour.

3. Mix the butternut squash, onions, mushrooms and garlic with the oil and paprika on a baking tray.

4. Roast in the middle of the oven for approximately 30 minutes, lowering the heat to 220°C/425°F/Gas 7 after 15 minutes.

5. Remove the mushrooms and kombu from the broth and replace with the roasted vegetables from the oven.

6. Pour some of the liquid onto the baking tray and scrape up anything that's got stuck there – that's where all the flavour is. Add the liquid and bits to the pan.

7. Add the ginger and simmer covered with a lid for approximately 20 minutes.

8. Blend to a completely smooth broth with a stick blender or in a food processor (the latter often gives the best result as you want the broth to be completely smooth and extremely creamy). Add more water if the broth feels too thick.

9. Add the soy sauce, miso, rice vinegar, coconut oil and salt and blend again. Check the flavouring and either leave to cool or use straightaway.

TARE

The flavouring added to the ramen broth is known as the tare. It can be varied to infinity. There are no rules, you can mix in a little of what you fancy and chefs often compete to create the most innovative flavour combinations. They smoke, ferment and add acidity and salt to enhance the fairly neutral base broth. The most classic tares are soy sauce, miso or sea salt that are mixed with pork or chicken broth directly in the noodle bowl. But you can also flavour with spice paste, infused oil, spice salt, vinegar, citrus or plenty of other tasty things.

Fat also counts as tare. Fat is key in a good broth and from time to time, some broths need a bit extra. Chicken broth is the best example of how the fat content can vary depending on the quality of the ingredient. At some ramen places you can even choose the level of fat content in your broth. If you choose the highest level you can, as a Westerner, get a bit of a shock. A thick, smooth broth that is quite high in fat already, mixed together with small chunks of fat – that's usually my limit. But many people love to take it up a notch, especially the Japanese.

The tare is whisked into the broth directly in the bowl before you add the noodles. When you're at a ramen joint, sitting at the bar alongside the kitchen, you often see a whole load of bowls, jars and bottles with different flavourings that each add a unique character to the same base broth. That's why it's important not to flavour a broth too much when you cook it, but instead keep it pretty neutral so that it can be flavoured later, as it's served. There are a couple of exceptions, however; both the mushroom broth and kotteri veggie broth are flavoured towards the end of the cooking process.

CHICKEN OR PORK FAT

Chicken or pork fat is a staple ingredient for ramen chefs. You leave chicken skin and fat to slowly melt together with water in a pan in order to extract the fat, which you store in a small jar in the fridge, ready to be mixed into a steaming hot broth. The meat that's left over after taking off the skin and fat you can fry, boil or grill – and use for anything you like.

MAKES APPROXIMATELY 200–300ML/
7–10½FL OZ/SCANT 1¼–1⅔ CUPS

6 chicken thighs or 200g/7oz pork fat

1. If using chicken fat, pull the chicken skin off the thighs and pick all the fat from the meat. If using pork fat, slice it into chunks.

2. Place the skin and fat in a pan and add 400ml/ 14fl oz/1¾ cups water.

3. Bring to the boil and simmer uncovered for approximately 3 hours. Add more water if it boils dry. The fat and skin should be covered by liquid the whole time.

4. Strain the liquid, leave to cool and place in the fridge overnight.

5. The next day you can easily separate the fat from the liquid.

6. Melt the fat in a pan and pour into a small jar with a tight-fitting lid. Keeps for 1 week in the fridge, 2 months in the freezer.

SICHUAN CHILLI PASTE

Chinese Sichuan pepper, or the Japanese version, sancho pepper, is a very special spice. It is fragrant, peppery and so hot and spicy that it makes the tongue tingle and almost feel numb. It is also insanely delicious. Here the Sichuan spice melts into the hot broth and causes a warming spice explosion in the mouth.

MAKES APPROXIMATELY 200ML/7FL OZ/ SCANT I CUP

- 2 small onions, coarsely chopped
- 4 garlic cloves, coarsely chopped
- 15cm/6in ginger root, peeled and sliced
- 3 tbsp ground Sichuan pepper
- 2 star anise, ground
- 2½ tbsp crushed small dried red Asian chillies
- 4 tbsp fermented bean and chilli paste (tobanjan)
- 2 tbsp Japanese soy sauce
- 100ml/3½fl oz/scant ½ cup vegetable oil

1. Sweat all the ingredients in a frying pan for approximately 5 minutes, until the onion has softened.

2. Blend into a smooth spice paste.

3. Store in a jar with a tight-fitting lid. Top the jar with oil and the paste will be preserved for longer. Keeps for approximately I week in the fridge.

CHILLI OIL

To get the right heat for your ramen you should always have a bottle of this chilli oil at the ready. It can be used as a flavouring for broth, together with miso, or drizzled over any ramen as a topping. It's also incredibly tasty drizzled over a freshly baked pizza – just sayin'.

MAKES APPROXIMATELY 250ML/9FL OZ/ GENEROUS I CUP

- 200ml/7fl oz/scant I cup vegetable oil
- 2 tbsp sesame oil
- 3 tbsp Korean chilli powder (gochugaru)
- 1½ tbsp crushed small dried red Asian chillies
- 2 garlic cloves, crushed

1. Gently heat all the ingredients in a pan.

2. Remove from the heat and leave to cool. Leave to infuse for approximately I hour.

3. Remove one of the garlic cloves and blend the oil.

4. Pour the oil into a thoroughly cleaned bottle or jar with a tight-fitting lid.

5. Store in the fridge. Keeps for up to 6 months.

MAYU – BLACK GARLIC OIL

Charred or burnt garlic can be regarded as a no-no in Italian cooking, when you want the garlic to slowly flavour the olive oil or butter and not give off any of the bitterness that comes through when it's overheated. In Japan it's the other way round of course. Mayu is made from burnt garlic that has been charred in oil until black. The flavour isn't especially palatable on its own, but once added to tonkotsu broth it's a winning combination. Thick, smooth gelatinous broth that becomes one with the burnt garlic. It's immensely good.

MAKES APPROXIMATELY 250ML/9FL OZ/ GENEROUS 1 CUP

150ml/5fl oz vegetable oil

8 garlic cloves, finely grated

65g/2¼oz/scant ½ cup sesame oil

1. Heat the oil in a pan and sweat the garlic. It should brown slowly for approximately 15 minutes, until it's completely black.

2. Stir continuously. After some time the starch from the garlic will form a glue-like lump, keep on stirring and try to separate the garlic in the pan. Leave to simmer until the garlic is charred. It should be completely black and burnt.

3. Remove from the heat and blend together with the sesame oil until smooth. Store in a bottle or a jar with a tight-fitting lid in the fridge. Keeps fresh for up to 1 month in the fridge.

GARLIC PURÉE

Plenty of garlic is used when cooking ramen. So much so that you always know when someone has slurped down a tonkotsu with garlic for lunch. At ramen joints you will often find whole garlic cloves in a small jar with a garlic press alongside so that you can decide the amount of garlic for yourself. To get a milder and rounder sweetness I usually boil the garlic and make a purée.

MAKES APPROXIMATELY 200ML/7FL OZ/ SCANT 1 CUP

3 whole garlic bulbs, split and peeled

3 tbsp vegetable oil

1. Boil the garlic cloves in a pan of water for approximately 10 minutes, until softened.

2. Drain the garlic and blend into a smooth purée.

3. Transfer to a jar with a tight-fitting lid and top with the oil so that the purée doesn't oxidise or go off. Keeps for up to 1 week in the fridge.

BONITO SALT

Katsuobushi is dried, smoked Japanese tuna that resembles a compact, hard piece of wood. When it's sliced into thin, thin flakes, every little speck gives an enormous amount of flavour. It is especially good for flavouring chicken broth, as the smokiness from the tuna adds a bit of depth. The salt can, however, be used for more than just a topping or flavouring for a ramen broth – I like to sprinkle it on tempura or over a soft boiled egg, put it in a sandwich or use it in a salad dressing.

MAKES APPROXIMATELY 125G/4½OZ

10g/½oz/2 tsp bonito flakes (katsuobushi)

65g/2½oz/¾ cup salt

1. Crush the bonito flakes using a pestle and mortar or blend until fine with the salt. Store in a jar – this keeps for a long time.

MISO AND SESAME TARE

Sometimes I swap the miso in miso ramen or spicy miso ramen for this tare. The broth gets a little bit thicker and richer thanks to the sesame paste. Ridiculously tasty.

MAKES APPROXIMATELY 150ML/5FL OZ/ SCANT ⅔ CUP

3 tbsp white miso paste

3 tbsp red miso paste

3 tbsp Japanese sesame paste (neri goma)
    or tahini

1. Mix together the white and red miso pastes in a bowl. Stir in the sesame paste so that you get a smooth thick sauce. Store in a jar with a tight-fitting lid. Keeps fresh for about a week in the fridge.

FIVE-SPICE CHILLI PASTE

A spice paste with a good punch, containing five-spice and Chinese soy sauce. In addition to stirring it into broth, it also makes a nice rub for meat that you then braise in the oven.

4 tbsp rapeseed oil with neutral flavour

2 small onions, coarsely chopped

4 garlic cloves, coarsely chopped

10cm/4in ginger root, peeled and coarsely chopped

2 tbsp Chinese five-spice blend

1 tbsp crushed small dried red Asian chillies

3 tbsp Chinese soy sauce

3 tbsp rice vinegar

2 tsp salt

1. Heat the oil in a pan and fry the onion, garlic, ginger and spices until slightly softened.

2. Add the soy sauce, vinegar and salt. Leave until half the liquid has been absorbed.

3. Blend until smooth. Store in a jar with a tight-fitting lid. Keeps for a few weeks in the fridge.

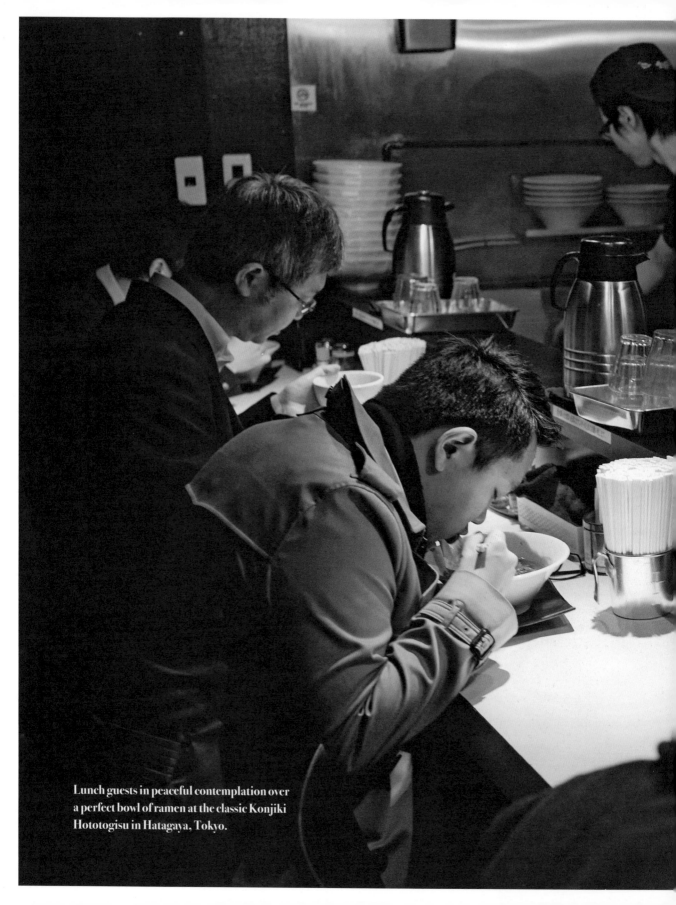

Lunch guests in peaceful contemplation over a perfect bowl of ramen at the classic Konjiki Hototogisu in Hatagaya, Tokyo.

NOODLES

NOODLE MAKING IS A SCIENCE. There are even schools in China that offer three-year courses for mastering the noble art of making noodles. Indeed, most types of noodles eaten in Japan are thought to have originated in China.

Many people confuse ramen noodles with egg noodles. 'Genuine' ramen noodles are made only from wheat flour, water and a substance called kansui. Kansui is an alkaline agent that can be compared to baking powder and lye water. Once in contact with wheat flour and water, it causes the chemical compounds of gluten proteins in the flour to change, making the noodles more chewy and springy. You can see the reaction from the change in colour that occurs as soon as kansui is added and the dough turns yellow; this is a distinctive characteristic of ramen noodles. There are a lot of 'fake' noodles where the yellow colour is enhanced by adding turmeric or other colouring.

Kansui gives the thin noodles the springiness they need to be able to take the hot broth without becoming soggy and overcooked. The kansui also gives a certain flavour to the noodles; think soda water, a slight alkaline note – similar to when you add too much baking powder when making a cake. Kansui is, unfortunately, tricky to find in the shops, and is also quite difficult to source online. A clever trick is to use toasted baking powder instead – when baking powder is toasted in the oven, the chemical structure changes and it turns into an alkaline powder that is similar to kansui.

Unlike ramen, the thicker udon noodles are thought to have existed in Japanese cuisine for many hundreds of years. The dough is made from just wheat and water and is worked for an extremely long time to get the required bouncy, rubbery texture. It's said that the udon masters start their working day with a walk a few hours long. They walk and walk, often barefoot, on top of their dough. The masters know exactly how their body weight affects the dough and how long they need to knead before it's perfect.

The best way to succeed with udon at home is to start off working the dough in a mixer and then place the dough in a large plastic zip-seal food bag and start stomping. Fold the dough continuously: when it has flattened out you fold it into three layers and stamp on it again. This way it will become as supple as silk but tough as a rubber ball.

What's also fascinating about udon is its bright white colour, although it's pretty difficult to achieve that effect at home. When the masters make udon they use a special udon flour that is very finely ground and extremely white in colour.

Soba means buckwheat in Japanese. Buckwheat has been used for hundreds of years in Japanese cooking. The traditional way of making the dough is to use 100 percent buckwheat; these noodles are called juwari soba. Boiling water is poured over the dough to make it a bit easier to work. The flour needs to be ground just before use and preferably from young buckwheat. You can also make soba from a combination of buckwheat and wheat flour; this is called ni-hachi soba. I use a ratio of about twice the amount of buckwheat to wheat flour. This makes the dough relatively easy to work, but you still have to be fast as it dries out quickly, and when it does it will no longer hold together.

RAMEN NOODLES

The dough needs to be worked thoroughly and it takes a long time before it comes together, so it's best to use a food mixer with a dough hook. Don't despair, it will look dry and crumbly at first but it will get more supple as you work it. If you haven't got a machine that can do the job you will have to work with your hands and arms, which I usually do anyway after the dough has come together in the machine. You will also need a pasta machine.

SERVES 12–16

2½ tsp toasted baking powder (see recipe to the right) or kansui

500ml/17fl oz/generous 2 cups cold water

1 tbsp salt

500g/1lb 2oz/4 cups strong white bread flour

550g/1lb 4oz/heaped 4⅓ cups tipo 00 flour

cornflour or potato flour, for rolling

1. Mix the baking powder and water in a bowl. Stir thoroughly until the baking powder has dissolved. Add the salt and stir until dissolved.

2. Combine the flours in the bowl of a food mixer and work in the liquid with the dough hook on a low speed until you get a firm dough – about 15 minutes. The dough should feel rubbery and very firm. If it hasn't started to come together after 10 minutes, add 1–2 tbsp water and leave it to run for a bit longer.

3. Turn the dough out onto a work surface and work for another 5 minutes with your hands and elbows. The dough will be quite heavy and difficult to work.

4. Cover the bowl with clingfilm and leave to rest at room temperature for approximately 1 hour.

5. Flatten the dough and divide it into 16 equally sized portions, approximately 4–5cm/1½–1¾in.

6. Feed the dough through the pasta machine to make sheets of dough. I usually run it to level 4, which should make the noodles thin enough. If you like your noodles thicker, all you have to do is go for a higher setting. You will probably find your preference after a few attempts. Powder the sheets with cornflour.

7. Run through the machine to make noodles; ramen noodles are a little thinner while tsukemen are usually a bit wider. Sprinkle over some more cornflour. Batch together into noodle nests.

8. Boil the noodles in salted water on a rolling boil for about 45 seconds just before serving. The noodles will continue to cook in the broth. You will usually find your favourite texture after a few attempts, I like it when the noodles are soft but when there is still some bite left to them.

9. The noodles can be stored wrapped in plastic in the fridge for up to 4 days or in the freezer for up to 6 months. Very suitable for making a big batch.

TOASTED BAKING POWDER

MAKES ABOUT 55G/2OZ/SCANT ½ CUP

55g/2oz/scant ½ cup baking powder

1. Preheat the oven to 140°C/275°F/Gas 1.

2. Spread out the baking powder on a baking tray. It's important that the tray is completely clean from any burnt fat or oil; if it's not, line it with baking paper.

3. Toast the baking powder in the middle of the oven for 1 hour.

4. Leave to cool and store in a jar with a tight-fitting lid. Keeps for a long time.

UDON NOODLES

Udon noodles are really thick noodles with a hefty, chewy bounce. The texture is achieved by working the dough for a long time. It's best to boil the noodles straight away as they turn a bit dull both in colour and texture from being stored too long in the fridge. Parboiling the noodles won't work either – they will lose their nice chewy texture.

SERVES 4–6

500g/1lb 2oz/4 cups wheat flour with high protein content, e.g. strong white bread flour
250ml/9fl oz/generous 1 cup water
½ tbsp salt
cornflour, for rolling

1. Combine the flour, water and salt in a food mixer.

2. Run the machine with a dough hook until you've got a dough.

3. Place the dough into a large plastic food bag with a zip-seal.

4. Remove your socks (make sure your feet are clean). Stamp on the dough until it is flat in the bag. Open and fold the dough twice. Stamp again.

5. Continue with the same procedure for 15 minutes. Change the bag once to make sure it doesn't split. The dough should be smooth, rubbery and elastic.

6. Sprinkle the worktop with sifted cornflour. Roll the dough until it's about 2–3mm/1/16–1/8in thick and about 20 x 40cm/8 x 16in in size.

7. Sift over cornflour and fold the dough four times.

8. Slice the dough into noodles about 5mm/1/4in wide. Fold them out and sprinkle with cornflour.

9. Boil in salted water for about 2 minutes.

10. The noodles can be served hot in a broth or cold (cool them down in iced water straight after boiling).

SOBA NOODLES

It's not easy to get soba noodles right, but remember that they don't have to be perfect, and that it will be worth the effort. The wheat flour helps the dough to stick together, since the buckwheat doesn't include any gluten and has a tendency to crumble otherwise.

SERVES 4–6

300g/10½oz/2/3 cups buckwheat flour
150g/5oz/scant 1¼ cups strong white bread flour
280ml/4fl oz/generous 1 cup boiling water
cornflour, for rolling

1. Mix the flours together in a bowl. Add the boiling water and work into a dough.

2. Turn the dough out onto a work surface and work with your hands and knuckles into a smooth dough. Add more wheat flour if the dough is sticky, or a little water if it seems too dry. Work the dough until if feels supple and firm, for approximately 10 minutes. It should be fairly firm.

3. Press out the dough onto the work surface. Rub the top and bottom with cornflour.

4. Roll out until approximately 30 x 30cm/12 x 12in in size and about 2mm/1/16in thick. Make sure the dough doesn't get too thin, or the noodles will break easily. Sift over cornflour as you roll it, flipping the dough over twice during rolling. Use your arms for this as the dough will break easily if you grab it with your hands.

5. Fold the dough until you have a four layers.

6. Slice into thin noodles with a knife with a straight blade. Sift over more cornflour so that the noodles don't stick together.

7. Boil the noodles immediately in salted boiling water, for 60 seconds maximum.

Wide udon noodles and thinner
soba noodles.

TOPPING

All components are of equal importance in a bowl of ramen and it's from the topping that you get the proteins in an otherwise fairly carb-packed dish. The most classic toppings are pork, egg, spring onion, beansprouts and bamboo shoots. Usually a fairly fatty cut of pork is used, for example belly or collar, that is braised for hours until tender and delicious. Chashu pork is the most traditional of them all. It is marinated in soy sauce, mirin, ginger and garlic and gives a fantastic salty-sweet caramel flavour with fat and pork rind that breaks apart in the broth – incredibly delicious.

Tip: if you have any leftover meat you can use it as a filling in steamed pork buns. I usually keep buns in the freezer ready to take out, steam and then fill with sliced chashu pork, hoisin sauce, Sriracha sauce, cucumber and lettuce. Or I use a few slices in a bánh mì sandwich with fermented carrot, daikon, cucumber and coriander.

In Japan it's also common to be served a fish cake on top of your ramen – a small white slice with a pink pattern or rim. The 'cake' is made from fish and shellfish paste and gives the broth a subtle fish flavour. I am, however, no fan of this cake, which is not dissimilar to crab sticks.

I love eggs, on the other hand, and think they are one of the most important toppings. I serve ramen with eggs that are poached, soy sauce pickled, soft boiled or cooked to 64°C/145°F. Nothing beats an egg that is bobbing up and down in the broth together with the noodles. It's also nice to add a raw egg yolk. You can, of course, serve your ramen without eggs but there is something special about that creamy yolk and soy sauce pickled white that really lifts the dish to new heights.

SOY SAUCE PICKLED EGGS

You need to plan ahead when making pickled eggs. Salt and sugar pickle the eggs so that the white gets a slightly harder consistency and the yolk becomes perfectly creamy. The ultimate time to leave the eggs to pickle for is one day before serving. But they are fine for up to three days. If they are left for longer they will get too pickled and become hard and rubbery in texture – not nearly as nice.

MAKES 6

6 eggs
100ml/3½fl oz/scant½ cup water
100ml/3½fl oz/scant ½ cup Japanese soy sauce
3¼ tbsp mirin
1 tbsp coarsely chopped ginger root

1. Soft boil the eggs: bring a pan of water to the boil and add the eggs, then lower the heat slightly and boil for 6 minutes. It's important that the eggs are just soft boiled. You'll want a runny egg yolk that gets pickled from the tasty marinade. An egg that's boiled too hard will be dull and almost ruin the dish, despite tasty noodles and broth.

2. Rinse the eggs in cold water until completely cooled down.

3. Bring the water, soy sauce, mirin and ginger to the boil. Simmer for approximately 5 minutes.

4. Leave to cool and pour into a jar. Peel the eggs and add to the marinade.

5. Store in the fridge for at least 10 hours and ideally up to 1 day before serving.

Eggs pickled for one day and three days respectively. There is a significant difference both in the white and the yolk.

CHASHU PORK

A ramen made from pork broth would be nothing without chashu pork on the top. The pork, either belly or collar, is roasted slowly with soy sauce, sweet mirin, ginger and onion. Both soy sauce and mirin add a hint of caramel to the fat – it's delicious. There are different kinds of chashu; you either roast the pork belly as it is or make a roll from pork belly or collar and slice it into rounds, so you can clearly see the stripes of fat surrounded by tender marinated meat. There are also different schools of thought for how to cook your chashu. Some boil it together with the broth first and then add it to a marinade. I don't think this gives the meat the same delicious flavour, so instead I recommend the method below, where you braise the meat in the marinade. Alternatively, if you make your broth with pork belly, you can use the leftover meat as topping by tearing it up like pulled pork and frying it off with some soy sauce, mirin and sesame – perfect if you're in a rush and only have time for cooking the broth.

SERVES 4 – 6

200ml/7fl oz/scant 1 cup water

250ml/9fl oz/1 cup Japanese soy sauce

200ml/7fl oz/scant 1 cup mirin

3 whole spring onions

10cm/4in ginger root, sliced

3 garlic cloves, crushed

1.25kg/2lb 12oz pork belly

2 tsp salt

1. Preheat the oven to 150°C/300°F/Gas 2.

2. In a casserole dish or a deep ovenproof dish, mix together the water, soy sauce and mirin. Add the spring onions, ginger, garlic and salt.

3. If the pork rind still has hair on it, burn it off with a blowtorch or remove with a shaver. Sounds extreme but you don't want spiky hairs in the meat.

4. *Whole pork belly:* place the pork with the rind facing down in the liquid (the meat will be about half covered in liquid.)

   Rolled pork belly: cut off some of the rind, leaving a quarter of it along one edge. Roll the meat so that the part with the rind is on the outside as a protective layer around the meat. Tie the roll up with cooking string. Add to the liquid.

   Pork collar: slice up the pork collar to flatten it out and then roll it up and tie with cooking string. Add to the liquid.

5. Cover the pork with a lid or aluminium foil and place in the bottom of the oven. Lower the heat to 130°C/250°F/Gas 1.

6. *Whole pork belly:* roast for 3 hours. Take out the dish and turn the meat over so that the rind faces upwards. Roast for another hour.

   Rolled pork belly: roast for 4 hours. Turn the meat over three times so that all sides of the rind lie face down in the marinade once.

   Pork collar: roast for 4 hours. Turn the meat over halfway through cooking so that both sides of the meat lie face down.

7. Take the meat out of the oven and leave to cool in the liquid. Cover and refrigerate overnight.

8. Before serving, cut the meat into thin slices and heat in the oven at 200°C/400°F/Gas 6 for 5 minutes maximum. Char with a blowtorch, if you like, to add more flavour and colour.

BBQ PORK

Ramen topped with a slice of meat infused with flavours from a charcoal grill is something extra special. The delicious BBQ flavour gives it another dimension. Here, the pork collar is slowly roasted in the oven with soy sauce, tomato purée, vinegar and sugar.

SERVES 4–6

800g/1lb 12oz pork collar

2 tsp salt

2 tbsp (2.5g) bonito flakes (katsuobushi)

2 tbsp tomato purée

2 tbsp Japanese soy sauce

2 tbsp rice vinegar

1 tbsp granulated sugar

1 garlic clove, peeled

2 tbsp finely chopped ginger root

200ml/7fl oz/scant 1 cup blonde lager

1. Preheat the oven to 130°C/250°F/Gas 1.

2. Season the pork collar all over with salt.

3. Place the bonito flakes, tomato purée, soy sauce, vinegar, sugar, garlic and ginger in a pan and boil for about 5 minutes.

4. Blend into a smooth purée and rub into the pork collar.

5. Place the pork on a baking tray and pour over the lager. Cover with foil and roast in the middle of the oven for approximately 4 hours.

6. Remove the foil and turn the heat up to 180°C/350°F/Gas 4. Roast for another 30 minutes.

7. Remove the pork collar from the oven. If you've got access to a grill it's nice to grill the meat on both sides to get a BBQ flavour.

64-DEGREE EGGS – ONSEN TAMAGO

The Japanese have been cooking perfect poached eggs for hundreds of years. Onsen tamago are prepared by placing eggs in nets, lowering them into hot volcanic springs and leaving them to cook slowly in their shells for 30–60 minutes, depending on the texture required. Traditionally, the eggs are served in a small bowl with dashi broth or soy sauce with mirin and spring onion. Nowadays, they are served with all kinds of dishes around the world. Nothing beats the soft, round egg with light white casing that hides a perfectly cooked yolk. Here's how to cook an onsen egg without a hot volcanic spring.

1. You will need a sous vide, precision cooker or a steam oven.

2. Set the temperature to 0.5 degrees Celsuis more than the temperature you'd like your egg to be. So for a 63°C/145°F degree egg, the thermometer should be set to 63.5°C/146°F.

3. Lower the eggs into the warm water or place them in a steam oven. Cook for 50 minutes, then rinse in cold water to halt the cooking process. If the egg is to be served warm it can be lowered into 80°C/176°F water for about 2 minutes before serving.

4. The easiest way to crack the egg is to tap the middle of the egg with a small knife and then crack it over your food or onto a side plate.

SOY SAUCE PICKLED EGG YOLKS

When you pickle only the egg yolk it becomes creamy, almost like a dollop of mayonnaise, thanks to the salty-sweet marinade that seeps into the egg. The ultimate pickling time is about eight hours, after which time the yolk will be perfectly creamy. It can pickle in the marinade for up to three days but the texture will become very firm and hard, in which case the yolk should be crumbled over the dish as a topping instead. I serve soy sauce pickled egg yolk with almost everything. On top of a sandwich with heaps of dry-cured ham and parsley, in a Taiwanese bao bun with slow cooked pork, in fried rice, as a topping for 'clearing out the fridge' hash with Sriracha sauce, or with Korean bibimbap. When I tried it with ice-cold wheat noodles and hot tsukemen broth, I realised it was an unbeatable combo.

MAKES 4

    50ml/1¾fl oz/generous 3 tbsp Japanese soy sauce
    50ml/1¾fl oz/generous 3 tbsp mirin
    4 egg yolks

1. Mix the soy sauce and mirin together in a small bowl or plastic container.
2. Add the egg yolks to the mixture and spoon over the marinade.
3. Cover with clingfilm and leave to stand for approximately 8 hours before serving.

ROAST TOMATOES

It can seem a bit strange to top an Asian dish with tomatoes, but it's actually a common ingredient in the modern Japanese kitchen. I was served roasted tomatoes in a ramen for the first time at one of the best ramen restaurants in New York – Ivan Ramen. Ivan Orkin, the chef, opened his first ramen place in Tokyo where he lived for many years with his Japanese wife. His ramen was a bit more experimental than the classic Japanese version, with smoked paprika and toppings such as roasted tomatoes. The tomato goes very well with broth and noodles and gives a mild, sweet acidity as a result of the roasting which concentrates the flavours. You can top any ramen with tomato but I think it goes particularly well with a classic shio, a cold dashi with cold noodles or a dashi with udon.

MAKES 12

    6 tomatoes, halved
    salt

1. Preheat the oven to 100°C/200°F/Gas ½.
2. Place the tomatoes with the cut side facing upwards on a baking tray covered in baking parchment. Sprinkle with salt.
3. Roast the tomatoes in the middle of the oven for approximately 4 hours, until the surface has dried slightly and some of the liquid has steamed off. It will make the flavours a bit more concentrated. Open the oven door a few times during the roasting to release steam.
4. Serve as a topping for ramen or udon dishes. The roasted tomatoes keep for up to 4 days in the fridge.

JAPANESE SPICE MIX – SHICHIMI TOGARASHI

A Japanese spice mix that you often find ready-mixed in a jar. The ingredients vary but Sichuan pepper, chilli and sesame seeds are key.

MAKES APPROXIMATELY 100ML/3½FL OZ

2 tbsp Sichuan pepper

2 tbsp Korean chilli powder (gochugaru)

1 tbsp crushed small dried red Asian chillies

1 piece of dried bitter orange peel, finely grated

1 tsp ground ginger

1 sheet nori seaweed

1 tsp black poppy seeds

1 tbsp toasted sesame seeds, preferably black and white

1. Blend all the spices apart from the sesame seeds together into a finely ground spice mix, or use a pestle and mortar.

2. Add the sesame seeds and crush coarsely, there should still be some whole seeds in the mix.

DEEP-FRIED SHALLOTS

Perfect sprinkled over ramen.

SERVES 4

300ml/10½fl oz/1¼ cups vegetable oil

4 shallots, finely sliced

salt

1. Heat the oil to 150°C/300°F.

2. Deep fry the shallots for about 5 minutes, until golden brown and crispy. Leave to drain on kitchen paper. Sprinkle with salt.

FURIKAKE

An addictive mix. Nice for sprinkling over boiled rice, salad, avocado sandwiches, soup, or for using as a topping for ramen.

MAKES APPROXIMATELY 250ML/9FL OZ/ GENEROUS 1 CUP

300ml/10½fl oz/1¼ cups vegetable oil

3 shallots, finely sliced

3 nori sheets

2 tbsp bonito flakes (katsuobushi)

30g/1oz/scant ¼ cup toasted sesame seeds, preferably black and white

2 tsp salt flakes

1. Heat the oil to 150°C/300°F. Deep fry the shallots for about 5 minutes, until golden brown and crispy. Don't increase the heat, or the shallots will burn. Leave to drain on kitchen paper.

2. Put the nori sheets, bonito flakes, half of the sesame seeds and the salt in a food processor or spice blender. Add the shallots and blend quickly – they should be fairly coarse.

3. Mix together with the remaining sesame seeds. Store in a jar.

MISE EN PLACE

WHEN SERVING RAMEN IT'S ALL ABOUT ADDING the components into one and the same bowl – broth, tare, noodles and topping. To make the process as smooth as possible and to make sure all the ingredients are ready at the same time you need good planning and mise en place.

Broths need boiling, meat braising and eggs pickling. Often you have to start the preparations the day before the eating. Therefore, always read through the recipe thoroughly and well in advance so that you have enough time to shop for ingredients and for the actual cooking.

I usually keep broth that I've made in advance in the freezer, but if I know that I'm having a few friends over for ramen on a Friday, I cook the broth on the Wednesday or the Thursday. If it's tonkotsu – the pork broth that needs at least 12 hours of cooking – I start it the weekend before and keep it in the fridge or freezer.

If I haven't got noodles in the freezer, I often make them the day or the weekend before. They will keep fresh for a week in the fridge and for up to five months in the freezer. I leave the meat in the oven overnight on the Wednesday or the Thursday and pickle the eggs on the Thursday evening so that they pickle for about 12 hours, which I think gives the best result. Sometimes I cook more meat than I need and freeze it once braised so it's ready for the next ramen dinner.

Check if you've got what you need for the dish you're cooking at home in the cupboard so that you've got enough time to shop for the ingredients you require.

If you're short on time for making the broth itself, choose a simpler broth that takes less time to cook – chicken, dashi or veggie, for example.

A short time ahead of serving, make sure spring onions are chopped, sesame seeds toasted, tare (flavouring) prepared, noodles defrosted or freshly made, the broth is taken out of the freezer and that you've got enough serving bowls out of the cupboard. Then when it's time to assemble the dish, you've got everything at hand and all you have to do is add all the elements to the bowls.

~~~~~~~~~~

HOW TO ASSEMBLE A RAMEN BOWL

1. Bring the water for the noodles to the boil, giving yourself ample time to do so.
2. Heat the broth and season to taste with salt depending on which tare (flavouring) you're using.
3. Slice the meat and heat in the oven.
4. Fill the bowls with hot water so that they are hot before adding the broth.
5. Discard the water and whisk together some of the broth and the tare directly in the bowls.
6. Boil the noodles and shake off the water thoroughly. Add the noodles to the bowls and lift them a little in the broth to make sure they don't stick together, then top with more broth.
7. Finish off by adding the topping.
8. Serve the bowls immediately after assembling. If left to stand for a couple of minutes the broth will get cold and the noodles overcooked.

002
RAMEN

As with other cheap fast food that can be made with great care and quality, ramen has become incredibly popular. Just like authentic pizza, BBQ and burgers, it's a dish that people love to rave about: there are endless top lists and blogs and you always find long queues outside the best places. Unlike other Japanese cuisine, there aren't that many rules when it comes to ramen; instead it's open to interpretation. Pictured here is comfort food at its best: a bowl with steaming hot broth and noodles for when it's a bit nasty outside. At the cheap ramen bars everyone is gathered, from businessmen and shop assistants to teenagers and miners. You eat quickly with your head lowered over the bowl while slurping loudly.

MISO RAMEN

Miso ramen is one of the classic ramen varieties. There is almost always a miso, a shio or a shoyu on the menu at ramen bars. These are often made from the same base broth but are flavoured with a different tare: miso, salt or soy sauce. I usually make my miso from pork and chicken broth and shio/shoyu from only chicken broth. But you can vary it depending on what you've got at home. I think it's tastiest to mix together two different kinds of miso paste, half white and half red. There is an infinite number of different kinds of miso in Japan but I can only get my hands on a maximum of five, all with different character, sweetness and saltiness. The red has slightly more depth than the white but you need the white to get a good balance in your broth.

SERVES 4

 1.8 litres/3 pints/7½ cups pork and chicken broth, see page 22

 2 tbsp red miso paste

 2 tbsp white miso paste

 2 tsp finely grated ginger

 4 portions ramen noodles, see page 38

 salt

TOPPING

 400g/14oz chashu pork, see page 45

 180g/6¼oz fresh beansprouts

 100g/3½oz mangetout, shredded

 2 small pak choi, diced

 3 spring onions, finely shredded

 4 soy sauce pickled eggs, see page 42

1. Preheat the oven to 200°C/400°F/Gas 6.

2. Slice the chashu pork thinly and arrange in portions of 3 slices on a baking tray.

3. Bring a large pan of salted water to the boil.

4. Blanch the beansprouts, mangetout and pak choi in the water for 30 seconds maximum. Remove them with a sieve so that you can save the water for boiling the noodles. Rinse the vegetables in cold water.

5. Bring the broth to the boil in a separate pan and lower the heat. Whisk the miso and ginger together in a bowl. Season to taste with salt.

6. Fill four bowls with hot water to warm them – this will keep the ramen warmer for longer. Discard the water when it's time to plate up.

7. Place the tray with the meat in the oven for 5 minutes. You could char the meat with a blowtorch afterwards to enhance the colour and flavour.

8. Divide the miso mixture between the four bowls, add the broth and whisk together.

9. Boil the noodles in the pan of water for about 45 seconds on a rolling boil. It's best to use a noodle basket or a sieve so that you can quickly take out the noodles once done. You only have a window of a few seconds to make sure they're not under- or overcooked. Drain thoroughly and transfer the noodles to the broth bowls.

10. Top with the beansprouts, mangetout, pak choi and spring onion.

11. Finish off with the chashu pork and halved eggs.

TANTANMEN RAMEN

Tantanmen is one kind of ramen that retains most if its Chinese roots. The dish is topped with minced pork, and the fermented bean and chilli paste together with the sesame paste makes an extremely flavourful broth. I like the super-thick variety, jam-packed with sesame, but then you have to be prepared for a ramen coma!

SERVES 4

1.8 litres/3 pints/7½ cups pork and chicken broth
  see page 22

8–12 tbsp Japanese sesame paste (neri goma)
  or tahini

4 tbsp chilli oil, see page 29

4 portions ramen noodles, see page 38

salt

CRISPY PORK MINCE

2 tbsp vegetable oil

400g/14oz pork mince

2 spring onions, finely shredded

1½ tbsp finely grated ginger root

1 garlic clove, finely grated

2 tbsp fermented bean and chilli paste (tobanjan)

1 tsp sesame oil

2 tbsp Japanese soy sauce

TOPPING

2 small pak choi, leaves picked

180g/6¼oz fresh beansprouts

4 spring onions, finely shredded

4 soy sauce pickled eggs, see page 42

4 tbsp toasted sesame seeds, crushed

1. Bring the broth to the boil in a pan and simmer over a low heat.

2. Bring a large pan of salted water to the boil.

3. Blanch the pak choi in the boiling water for about 30 seconds, then dip in the beansprouts quickly. Remove the vegetables with a sieve so that you don't have to drain all the water and boil new for the noodles. Rinse the vegetables immediately in cold water, they should still be very crunchy.

4. Heat the oil in a frying pan and fry the mince together with the spring onions, ginger and garlic. Add the fermented bean and chilli paste, sesame oil and soy sauce. Fry until the mince has coloured nicely and is crispy.

5. Fill four bowls with hot water to warm them. Discard the water when it's time to plate up.

6. Whisk a quarter of the sesame paste and chilli oil together in each bowl. Add the broth and stir.

7. Boil the noodles for approximately 45 seconds in the pan of water on a rolling boil. It's best to use a noodle basket or a sieve so that you can reuse the water and quickly take out the noodles once done. You only have a window of a few seconds to make sure they're not under- or overcooked. Drain thoroughly and transfer the noodles to the broth bowls.

8. Top with the mince, pak choi, beansprouts, spring onion and pickled eggs.

9. Serve sprinkled with the sesame seeds.

SPICY MISO RAMEN

A hot version of the delicious, salty, opaque broth in a classic miso ramen. The heat comes from the chilli oil, which can be added to suit your taste. Wherever you eat miso it's usually topped with sweetcorn. This way of serving originated from Hokkaido where miso ramen is topped with sweetcorn and a knob of butter. I fry sweetcorn, preferably fresh, in a really hot frying pan until it becomes slightly charred, and this adds flavour to the whole dish. Sometimes I swap miso for miso and sesame tare, see page 31, for a more intense and flavourful broth.

SERVES 4

3 tbsp white miso paste

3 tbsp red miso paste

4 tbsp chilli oil, shop bought or homemade, see page 29

1½ tbsp finely grated ginger root

1.8 litres/3 pints/7½ cups pork and chicken broth, see page 22

4 portions ramen noodles, see page 38

salt

TOPPING

12 thin slices chashu pork, see page 45

2 fresh corn on the cob, or 150g/5½oz/1 cup frozen sweetcorn kernels

1 tbsp vegetable oil

180g/6¼oz fresh beansprouts

4 spring onions, shredded

120g/4¼oz fresh spinach

4 soy sauce pickled eggs, see page 42

1. Preheat the oven to 200°C/400°F/Gas 6.

2. Slice the chashu pork thinly and arrange into portions of 3 slices on a baking tray.

3. Bring a large pan of salted water to the boil.

4. Mix the miso pastes, chilli oil and ginger together in a small bowl.

5. Cut off the corn from the cobs. Heat the oil in a frying pan and toast the corn until just starting to char. Add salt.

6. Blanch the beansprouts in the pan of boiling water for about 30 seconds, using a sieve or a noodle basket to remove them. Rinse in cold water.

7. Fill four bowls with hot water to warm them. Discard the water when it's time to plate up.

8. Place the tray with the meat in the oven for 5 minutes. You could char the meat with a blowtorch afterwards to enhance the colour and flavour.

9. Divide the miso mixture between the four bowls, add the broth and whisk together.

10. Boil the noodles for approximately 45 seconds in the pan of water on a rolling boil. It's best to use a noodle basket or a sieve so that you can reuse the water and quickly take out the noodles once done. You only have a window of a few seconds to make sure they're not under- or overcooked. Drain thoroughly and transfer the noodles to the broth bowls.

11. Top with the pork, sweetcorn, beansprouts, spring onion, spinach and eggs.

12. Serve with more chilli oil if you want; some like a gentle heat while others like it almost too hot to bear.

KIMCHI RAMEN

Deep-fried, slow-cooked pork belly that is crispy on the outside and has a sweet caramel flavour is one of the most delicious things ever. If you haven't got time to make 64-degree eggs, use poached or boiled eggs instead.

SERVES 4

> 6 tbsp Korean chilli paste (gochujang)
>
> 4 tsp grated ginger root
>
> 4 tbsp Japanese soy sauce
>
> 1.8 litres/3 pints/7½ cups pork and chicken broth, see page 22
>
> 4 portions ramen noodles, see page 38

GINGER BRAISED PORK

> 300ml/10½fl oz/1¼ cups blonde lager
>
> 200ml/7fl oz/scant 1 cup mirin
>
> 2 tbsp demerara sugar
>
> 100ml/3½fl oz/scant ½ cup Japanese soy sauce
>
> 2 tbsp Korean chilli powder (gochugaru)
>
> 3 tbsp finely grated ginger root
>
> 2 spring onions
>
> 3 garlic cloves, crushed
>
> 600g/1lb 5oz pork belly
>
> salt
>
> oil for deep frying

TOPPING

> 200g/7oz kimchi
>
> 4 x 64-degree eggs, see page 46, or poached eggs
>
> 120g/4¼oz fresh beansprouts
>
> 4 spring onions, finely shredded
>
> crushed sesame seeds, preferably black and white

1. Preheat the oven to 150°C/300°F/Gas 2.

2. Start with the pork: mix the lager, mirin, sugar, soy sauce, Korean chilli powder, ginger, spring onion and garlic in a pan or a deep ovenproof dish.

3. Salt the pork belly and place in the dish with the rind facing down. Cover with a lid or aluminium foil. Turn the oven down to 130°C/250°F/Gas 1. Roast in the middle of the oven for 2½ hours.

4. Turn the meat over and roast for another hour. Remove the lid and increase the heat to 180°C/350°F/Gas 4. Roast for another 20 minutes. Take the meat out of the oven and leave to cool.

5. Fill four bowls with hot water to warm them. Discard the water when it's time to plate up.

6. Bring a large pan of salted water to the boil. Heat the oil for the deep frying to 180°C/350°F.

7. Dice the braised meat. Deep fry in the oil for approximately 3 minutes, until the rind crackles and is crispy. Leave to drain on kitchen paper.

8. Heat the broth in a pan. Divide the Korean chilli paste, ginger and soy sauce between the four bowls, add the hot broth and whisk together.

9. Boil the noodles for approximately 45 seconds in the pan of water on a rolling boil. It's best to use a noodle basket or a sieve so that you can quickly take out the noodles once done. You only have a window of a few seconds to make sure they're not under- or overcooked. Drain thoroughly and transfer the noodles to the broth bowls.

10. Top with the kimchi, deep-fried pork, egg, beansprouts and spring onion. Sprinkle over the sesame seeds.

TONKOTSU RAMEN

The king of ramen broths and one that should cook for a long, long time. I have been served tonkotsu that's been boiling for anything from 10 to 48 hours. There are no shortcuts here! The broth needs at least 10 hours to get even close to good. When the broth is boiled for this long, the collagen is released from the pig's trotters, which gives a lovely gelatinous texture to the broth, making it sticky, thick and smooth. Sure, you can make this ramen with ready-made noodles, but everything else should preferably be from scratch and homemade. A common flavouring is black garlic oil. The slightly bitter and burnt note goes surprisingly well with the smooth, mild and meaty broth.

SERVES 4

1.8 litres/3 pints/7½ cups tonkotsu broth, see page 25

4 tbsp garlic purée, see page 30

4 portions ramen noodles, see page 38

TOPPING

400g/14oz chashu pork, see page 45

4 soy sauce pickled eggs, see page 42

8 tbsp finely shredded spring onion

4 tbsp black garlic oil, see page 30

toasted, ground sesame seeds

1. Preheat the oven to 200°C/400°F/Gas 6.

2. Slice the chashu pork thinly and divide into portions of 3 slices on a baking tray.

3. Bring a large pan of salted water to the boil for the noodles.

4. Warm the broth in a separate pan and add salt to taste.

5. Fill four bowls with hot water to warm them. Discard the water when it's time to plate up.

6. Divide the garlic purée between the four bowls and whisk in the broth.

7. Boil the noodles for approximately 45 seconds in the pan of water on a rolling boil. It's best to use a noodle basket or a sieve so that you can reuse the water and quickly take out the noodles once done. You only have a window of a few seconds to make sure they're not under- or overcooked. Drain thoroughly and transfer the noodles to the broth bowls.

8. Top with the chashu pork, pickled egg, spring onion, black garlic oil and sesame seeds.

YAKINIKU RAMEN

*You can't help but love the flavour of yakiniku –
chargrilled or fried rib eye steak with soy sauce, ginger,
sesame and onion. If you fry the meat, make sure to
use a really hot pan and fry it in batches to get the right
colour and flavour (don't worry if it gets a bit charred at
the edges). The meat tops a ramen made from chicken
broth flavoured with soy sauce. Chicken fat is added for
texture; it lifts all the flavours and sticks to the noodles.*

SERVES 4

    1.8 litres/3 pints/7½ cups chicken broth,
        see page 25

    6 tbsp Japanese soy sauce

    4 tbsp chicken fat, see page 28

    4 portions ramen noodles, see page 38

YAKINIKU

    400g/14oz rib eye steak, finely sliced

    1 tbsp vegetable oil

    2 tsp sesame oil

    4 tbsp Japanese soy sauce

    2 tbsp rice vinegar

    3 tbsp finely chopped ginger root

    2 spring onions, finely sliced

    2 garlic cloves, finely chopped

    200g/7oz fresh beansprouts

    1 tbsp toasted sesame seeds

TOPPING

    2 nori sheets, halved

    4 spring onions, finely sliced

    1 tbsp toasted sesame seeds

1. Heat up the broth in a pan.

2. Bring a large pan of salted water to the boil for
   the noodles.

3. Start with the yakiniku: mix the meat with the
   vegetable oil, sesame oil, soy sauce, vinegar, ginger
   and spring onion.

4. Heat up a frying pan or a wok and fry the meat
   in batches over a high heat together with all the
   marinade. Let the meat colour, it's the charred
   flavour that makes this dish. Add the garlic once the
   meat has coloured so that it doesn't get too burnt.

5. Add the beansprouts and sesame seeds, and leave
   to fry for a few minutes.

6. Fill four bowls with hot water so that the broth and
   noodles keep warm for longer. Discard the water
   when it's time to plate up.

7. Fill the bowls with hot broth. Add 1½ tbsp soy
   sauce and 1 tbsp chicken fat to each bowl and
   stir. Season to taste with salt and more soy sauce
   if needed.

8. Boil the noodles for approximately 45 seconds
   in the pan of water on a rolling boil. It's best to
   use a noodle basket or a sieve so that you can
   reuse the water and quickly take out the noodles
   once done. You only have a window of a few
   seconds to make sure they're not under- or
   overcooked. Drain thoroughly and transfer the
   noodles to the broth bowls.

9. Add the nori sheets to the broth and top the
   noodles with the meat and the spring onion and
   sesame seeds.

BEEF BONE RAMEN

A fairly delicate broth, flavoured only with soy sauce, vinegar and sesame oil. This is the opposite of the flavourful, thick kotteri broth. It's a transparent broth with thin slices of charred meat and onion as toppings. Unbelievably tasty.

SERVES 4

1.8 litres/3 pints/7½ cups beef bone broth, see page 26

450–600ml/¾–1 pint/2–2½ cups Japanese soy sauce

2 tbsp rice vinegar

1 tsp sesame oil

4 portions ramen noodles, see page 38

TOPPING

400g/14oz rib eye steak, or marbled steak

oil for frying

3 spring onions, finely sliced

deep-fried shallots, see page 48

toasted sesame seeds, preferably black and white

1. Halve the steak lengthways so that you end up with two thinner pieces.

2. Heat the oil over a high heat. Sear the meat all around so that only the surface gets coloured. Transfer to a plate and leave to rest.

3. Bring a large pan of salted water to the boil for the noodles.

4. Fill four bowls with hot water to warm them. Discard the water when it's time to plate up.

5. Heat the broth in a pan.

6. Slice the meat thinly with a newly sharpened knife. The slices should be super thin.

7. Divide the soy sauce and rice vinegar between the four bowls and add a few drops of sesame oil. Ladle in the broth and mix together.

8. Boil the noodles for approximately 45 seconds in the pan of water on a rolling boil. It's best to use a noodle basket or a sieve so that you can reuse the water and quickly take out the noodles once done. You only have a window of a few seconds to make sure they're not under- or overcooked. Drain thoroughly and transfer the noodles to the broth bowls.

9. Top with a few slices of meat and the spring onion, deep-fried shallots and sesame seeds.

SHORT RIB RAMEN

This ramen dish really packs a punch. Beef short ribs are slowly braised in the oven with five-spice – a mix of cinnamon, star anise, cloves, fennel and Sichuan pepper.

MAKES 4 PORTIONS

    1.8 litres/3 pints/7½ cups beef bone broth, see page 26

    8 tbsp five-spice chilli paste, see page 31

    4 portions ramen noodles see page 38

FIVE-SPICE SHORT RIBS

    1kg/2lb 4oz short ribs or chuck

    100ml/3½fl oz/scant ½ cup Chinese black vinegar

    100ml/3½fl oz/scant ½ cup Japanese soy sauce

    3 tbsp Chinese mushroom soy sauce

    4 star anise

    1 cinnamon stick

    1½ tsp Sichuan pepper, crushed

    3 whole cloves

    1 tsp fennel seeds

    10cm/4in ginger root, sliced

    4 garlic cloves, crushed

    2 tbsp demerara sugar

TOPPING

    2 fresh corn on the cob or 80g/2¾oz/heaped ½ cup frozen sweetcorn kernels

    2 tbsp vegetable oil

    8 padrón peppers

    2 jalapeño peppers, sliced

    80g/2¾oz mizuna leaves or fresh spinach

    8 lemon slices

1. Preheat the oven to 130°C/250°F/Gas 1.

2. Place the meat in a deep ovenproof dish.

3. Mix together the rest of the ingredients for the five-spice short ribs and add to the dish. Cover with foil. Roast in the middle of the oven for 5 hours, until the meat is tender.

4. Heat the broth in a pan.

5. Cut the corn off the cobs. Heat the oil in a frying pan and fry the corn until it has coloured.

6. Remove the corn from the pan and fry the padrón peppers in the hot oil and a little salt. Set aside.

7. Bring a large pan of salted water to the boil for the noodles.

8. Fill four bowls with hot water to warm them. Discard the water when it's time to plate up.

9. Cut the meat into chunks against the bones. (You can warm the meat in a moderate oven if needed.)

10. Put 2 tbsp of the five-spice chilli paste in each noodle bowl, add the broth and whisk together.

11. Boil the noodles for approximately 45 seconds in the pan of water on a rolling boil. It's best to use a noodle basket or a sieve so that you can reuse the water and quickly take out the noodles once done. You only have a window of a few seconds to make sure they're not under- or overcooked. Drain thoroughly and transfer the noodles to the broth bowls.

12. Top with the meat, sweetcorn, padrón peppers, jalapeño peppers and mizuna.

13. Place two lemon slices against the edge of each bowl.

Shio ramen and
shoyu ramen

SHIO RAMEN

Shio means salt in Japanese. It's one of the most common ramen dishes and can be found in almost all ramen joints. A simple chicken broth is flavoured with sea salt and is topped with chashu pork, beansprouts and spring onion. The topping usually varies from place to place but the broth is always the same – only salted.

SERVES 4

1.8 litres/3 pints/7½ cups chicken broth,
    see page 25

4 tbsp sea salt

4 tbsp chicken fat, see page 28 (optional)

4 portions ramen noodles, see page 38

TOPPING

1 tbsp shredded, dried mushroom (black fungus)

400g/14oz chashu pork, see page 45

180g/6¼oz fresh beansprouts

6 spring onions, finely shredded

4 soy sauce pickled eggs, see page 42

1. Heat the broth in a pan.

2. Soak the dried mushrooms in boiling hot, salted water for approximately 15 minutes.

3. Preheat the oven to 200°C/400°F/Gas 6.

4. Slice the chashu pork thinly and arrange in portions of 3 slices on a baking tray. Heat in the top of the oven for approximately 5 minutes before serving. If you want you can also char the meat with a blowtorch, so that the fat is caramelised and the soy sauce marinade tastes even better.

5. Bring a large pan of salted water to the boil for the noodles.

6. Fill four bowls with hot water to warm them. Discard the water when it's time to plate up.

7. Blanch the beansprouts for 30 seconds in the pan of boiling water, remove with a sieve and rinse in cold water.

8. Ladle the broth into the bowls, and whisk 1 tbsp of the sea salt and 1 tbsp of the chicken fat (if using) into each bowl.

9. Boil the noodles for approximately 45 seconds in the pan of water on a rolling boil. It's best to use a noodle basket or a sieve so that you can reuse the water and quickly take out the noodles once done. You only have a window of a few seconds to make sure they're not under- or overcooked. Drain thoroughly and transfer the noodles to the broth bowls.

10. Top with the chashu pork, mushrooms, beansprouts, spring onions and egg halves.

SHOYU RAMEN

Shoyu means soy in Japanese and is a traditional ramen broth. It's a simple chicken broth that is mixed with Japanese soy sauce. The topping – chashu pork, beansprouts, bamboo shoots, and spring onion – is almost the same as for shio. Tokyo ramen is a type of shoyu ramen but is mostly made from chicken and pork broth, sometimes with a little dashi added for extra umami and complexity. Shoyu or Tokyo ramen are probably the most well known of all ramen and can almost always be found on the menu.

SERVES 4

    1.8 litres/3 pints/7½ cups chicken broth, see page 25 or pork and chicken broth, see page 22

    6 tbsp Japanese soy sauce

    4 tbsp chicken fat, see page 28 (optional)

    4 portions ramen noodles, see page 38

TOPPING

    400g/14oz chashu pork, see page 45

    1 x 150g/9oz jar bamboo shoots

    2 tbsp Japanese soy sauce

    1½ tbsp rice vinegar

    180g/6¼oz fresh beansprouts

    6 spring onions, finely shredded

    4 soy sauce pickled eggs, see page 42

1. Heat the broth in a pan.

2. Preheat the oven to 200°C/400°F/Gas 6.

3. Slice the meat thinly and arrange in portions of 3 slices on a baking tray. Heat in the top of the oven for approximately 5 minutes before serving. If you want you can also char the meat with a blowtorch, so that the fat is caramelised and the soy sauce marinade tastes even better.

4. Bring a large pan of salted water to the boil.

5. Halve the bamboo shoots lengthways, and mix together with the soy sauce and rice vinegar.

6. Fill four bowls with hot water so that the broth and noodles keep warm for longer. Discard the water when it's time to plate up.

7. Blanch the beansprouts for 30 seconds in the pan of boiling water, remove with a sieve and rinse in cold water.

8. Ladle the broth into the bowls, whisk 1½ tbsp of the soy sauce into each bowl and 1 tbsp of the chicken fat, if using.

9. Boil the noodles for approximately 45 seconds in the pan of water on a rolling boil. It's best to use a noodle basket or a sieve so that you can reuse the water and quickly take out the noodles once done. You only have a window of a few seconds to make sure they're not under- or overcooked. Drain thoroughly and transfer the noodles to the broth bowls.

10. Top with the chashu pork, bamboo shoots, beansprouts, spring onion and egg halves.

THE RAMEN STORY

IT'S NO SECRET THAT MANY people become addicted after their first bowl of noodles. When you enter a ramen bar in Tokyo or another large city you notice the variety of the clientele. There are teenagers, businessmen, street cleaners in work-wear, women and men, old and young – a mixed bag of people slurping away loudly next to each other.

Ramen hasn't actually been eaten in Japan for as long as you might think. Noodles have been around for a long time, but not the thin wheat noodles that are the signature ramen noodles made from water, flour and kansui. Historically the main ingredient was rice, not wheat. The dish was probably brought to Japan by Chinese merchants at the start of the 1920s. That's when the first small noodle trolleys and Chinese noodle cafés popped up wherever the Chinese sold their soba or shuka soba (noodles in broth), at a low cost. The dish was prepared and served by the Chinese and hadn't yet found its way into Japanese food traditions.

During the Second World War Japan was a country in turmoil. The people were starving and ingredients were hard to come by. Shina soba (or ramen, as we now know it) disappeared from the streets just like almost all other food. The Japanese lost the war in 1945 and the US occupied the country. During the occupation, food was sent to Japan from the US to help the starving Japanese. Most supplies were made up of wheat and pork, which led to these ingredients being used for cheap, filling dishes. Ramen with pork fat, pork-filled gyoza and okonomiyaki made from pork and cabbage became staple dishes during the crisis. Ramen therefore gained its current status in the lives of the Japanese. It provided the energy, nutrition and strength needed to build up the country again.

During the 1950s the name of the noodle soup changed from shina soba to ramen. Japanese war veterans opened ramen restaurants. The cheap and filling dish became food for the low-paid, and for men and women who worked hard for the country's recuperation and growth. Today you can still find ramen places that serve ramen rockabilly style: chefs with waxed hair dressed in 50s shirts who work listening to 50s rock.

Ramen is more than just a dish for the Japanese. It has become popular in its own right for its simplicity and incredible flavour. Visitors from all over the world have noticed the tender care that goes into the broth, noodles and flavourings. These same visitors have then gone on to open ramen bars in cities all over the world. And the two things that all these places have in common are the simplicity of the food and the diverse mix of customers who all love ramen.

GREEN CURRY RAMEN

The original Bassanova Ramen restaurant was in the suburb of Setagaya, just outside central Tokyo, but later the founder brought the concept to the US and it has now become a firm favourite with all ramen-eating New Yorkers. The place is situated in a small basement in Chinatown and they serve both half and whole portions of ramen. This means that you can try two different kinds of ramen or complement with gyoza or pork buns. Instead of traditional Japanese flavours, all the food has a touch of Thailand: spicy curry pastes and coconut.

SERVES 4

1.8 litres/3 pints/7½ cups chicken broth,
     see page 25

6 tbsp coconut cream

4 portions ramen noodles, see page 38

GREEN CURRY PASTE

6 garlic cloves, peeled

2 tbsp chopped galangal

1 tbsp coriander seeds

2 lemongrass stalks

5 dried kaffir lime leaves

10 small green bird's eye chillies or 5 green chillies

60g/2oz fresh coriander, with roots if possible

2 shallots

1½ tbsp fish sauce

TOPPING

300g/10½oz boiled chicken, possibly leftovers
     from the broth

3 tbsp rice vinegar

2 tbsp Japanese soy sauce

2 tsp sesame oil

8 Chinese long beans or 150 green beans

2 carrots, finely shredded

15cm/6in ginger root, finely shredded

1 bunch Thai basil

1 bunch coriander

1 batch deep-fried shallots, see page 48

1. Blend together all the ingredients for the curry paste in a food processor.

2. Tear the warm chicken into shreds and mix together with the vinegar, soy sauce and sesame oil.

3. Bring a large pan of salted water to the boil. Heat the broth in a separate pan.

4. Fill four bowls with hot water to warm them. Discard the water when it's time to plate up.

5. Blanch the beans in the boiling water for 1 minute, remove with a sieve and rinse in cold water.

6. Whisk together 1½ tbsp coconut cream and ½ tbsp of the green curry paste with a little of the broth in each of the bowls. Top up with more broth.

7. Boil the noodles for about 45 seconds in the pan of water on a rolling boil. It's best to use a noodle basket or a sieve so that you can reuse the water and quickly take out the noodles once done. You only have a window of a few seconds to make sure they're not under- or overcooked. Drain thoroughly and transfer the noodles to the broth bowls.

8. Top with the beans, carrots, ginger, herbs, a dollop of green curry paste and the chicken. Sprinkle over the fried shallots.

SPICY GARLIC RAMEN

Garlic slowly fried in oil until golden brown and deep in flavour is then mixed with miso, fermented bean and chilli paste and vinegar to flavour and thicken the neutral chicken broth – a perfect combo for the noodles. This ramen is topped with chicken – you can use the chicken from when you boiled the broth, or if you don't have any of that left, you can leave chicken thighs or fillets to boil in the broth when you heat it up.

SERVES 4

1.8 litres/3 pints/7½ cups chicken broth, see page 25

4 portions ramen noodles, see page 38

HOT GARLIC PASTE

100ml/3½fl oz/1¼ cups vegetable oil

6 garlic cloves, finely grated

3 tbsp sesame oil

3 tbsp fermented bean and chilli paste (tobanjan)

2 tbsp Japanese sesame paste (neri goma) or tahini

1½ tbsp rice vinegar

3 tbsp toasted sesame seeds

TOPPING

120g/4¼oz fresh beansprouts

300g/10½oz boiled chicken, possibly leftovers from the broth

3 tbsp chilli oil, see page 29

6 spring onions, finely sliced

2 tbsp coarsely chopped coriander

2 soft-boiled eggs

4 tbsp crushed black sesame seeds

1. For the garlic paste, heat up the oil to about 130°C/260°F. Add the garlic and leave to sizzle for approximately 10 minutes. It should go soft and shiny at first and then turn golden brown. After a while, the garlic will get quite sticky from the starch in the pan but keep on stirring. Remove the pan from the heat and add the sesame oil, bean and chilli paste, sesame paste and rice vinegar. Add the sesame seeds and blend coarsely.

2. Bring a large pan of salted water to the boil for the noodles. Heat the broth in a separate pan.

3. Fill four bowls with hot water to warm them. Discard the water when it's time to plate up.

4. Heat a little vegetable oil in a frying pan or a wok until really hot. Fry the beansprouts quickly over a high heat so that they become slightly charred. Remove from the heat and transfer to a bowl.

5. Cut the chicken into smaller chunks and heat in the frying pan together with the chilli oil.

6. Whisk together 2 tbsp of the garlic paste with 100ml (3½fl oz) of the broth in each bowl. Top up with more broth.

7. Boil the noodles for approximately 45 seconds in the pan of water on a rolling boil. It's best to use a noodle basket or a sieve so that you can reuse the water and quickly take out the noodles once done. You only have a window of a few seconds to make sure they're not under- or overcooked. Drain thoroughly and transfer the noodles to the broth bowls.

8. Top with the chicken, beansprouts, spring onion, coriander, egg halves and sesame seeds.

KOTTERI VEGGIE RAMEN

One hundred times more delicious than you can imagine. Lots of flavour, smooth consistency and a kick-ass topping of mushrooms fried in soy sauce. The aubergine plays an important part. It's grilled in the oven until it's completely black and brings a roasted, almost smoky flavour. You can vary the topping with different kinds of vegetables, mushrooms, tofu and egg.

SERVES 4

1 aubergine, halved lengthways

vegetable oil

1.6 litres/2¾ pints/6⅔ cups kotteri veggie broth,
    see page 27

2 tbsp chilli oil, see page 29

4 portions ramen noodles, see page 38

salt

TOPPING

20g/¾oz/2 tbsp shredded dried mushrooms
    (black fungus)

2 tbsp vegetable oil

2 tbsp Japanese soy sauce

2 tsp finely grated ginger

1 garlic clove, finely grated

2 corn on the cob or 90g/3oz/½ cup frozen
    sweetcorn kernels

100g/3½oz water spinach or standard spinach

3 spring onions, finely shredded

4 soy sauce pickled eggs, see page 42

1½ tbsp toasted sesame seeds, crushed

salt

1. Turn the grill to its highest setting.

2. Place the aubergine on a baking tray with the cut side facing up. Brush with oil and sprinkle with salt.

3. Grill in the middle of the oven for approximatley 30 minutes, until the aubergine is completely soft and has plenty of colour.

4. Place the dried mushrooms in a bowl of hot water. Leave to soak for about 30 minutes, then drain.

5. Heat 1 tbsp of the oil in a frying pan and sweat the mushrooms with the soy sauce and ginger for 5 minutes. Add the garlic towards the end. Don't let the mushrooms burn – turn down the heat if the pan gets too hot.

6. Cut the corn off the cobs. Heat the remaining tbsp oil in a pan and fry the corn over a fairly high heat until coloured. Sprinkle with salt.

7. Bring a large pan of salted water to the boil.

8. Fill four bowls with hot water to warm them. Discard the water when it's time to plate up.

9. Heat up the broth. If it feels too thick you can dilute it with a little water. It should be fairly thick but you should still be able to slurp it easily.

10. Blanch the spinach for about 30 seconds.

11. Ladle the broth into the bowls and stir ½ tbsp chilli oil and a quarter of the aubergine into each.

12. Boil the noodles for approximately 45 seconds in the pan of water on a rolling boil. It's best to use a noodle basket or a sieve so that you can quickly take out the noodles once done. Drain thoroughly and transfer the noodles to the broth bowls.

13. Top with the mushroom, sweetcorn, spring onion, spinach, egg halves and sesame seeds.

MUSHROOM TOFU RAMEN

A sumptuous mushroom broth with tofu, mushrooms
and sesame. This is a relatively delicate ramen dish
without spicy and complex flavours. If you want you can
stir a spoonful of Sichuan chilli paste or miso and sesame
tare (see page 31) into each bowl to get a thicker and
fuller flavour for your broth. Some variation can be nice
from time to time.

SERVES 4

    1.6 litres/2¾ pints/6⅔ cups mushroom broth,
        see page 26

    4 portions ramen noodles, see page 38

TOPPING

    1 tbsp vegetable oil

    200g/7oz fresh shiitake mushrooms

    300g/10½oz silken tofu, diced

    200g/7oz enoki mushrooms, separated

    80g/2¾oz mizuna leaves or fresh spinach

    1 batch deep-fried shallots, see page 48

    4 tbsp furikake, see page 48

    salt

1. Bring a large pan of salted water to the boil for
   the noodles.

2. Heat up the broth in a separate pan.

3. Fill four bowls with hot water to warm them.
   Discard the water when it's time to plate up.

4. Heat the oil in a frying pan and sweat the shiitake
   over a medium heat for about 5 minutes. Sprinkle
   with salt.

5. Ladle the broth into the bowls.

6. Boil the noodles for approximately 45 seconds
   in the pan of water on a rolling boil. It's best to
   use a noodle basket or a sieve so that you can
   reuse the water and quickly take out the noodles
   once done. You only have a window of a few
   seconds to make sure they're not under- or
   overcooked. Drain thoroughly and transfer the
   noodles to the broth bowls.

7. Top with the shiitake, tofu, (raw) enoki, mizuna or
   spinach, deep-fried shallots and furikake.

SICHUAN PORK RAMEN

Thick pork ribs that have been braised until tender with chilli, ginger and beer sit on top of a pork and chicken broth flavoured with Sichuan pepper, chilli and onion. Sichuan pepper has a fragrant flavour and a unique pepperiness that works really with the fatty pork and the salty broth. The broth gets a slightly syrupy consistency from the sesame paste and tare.

SERVES 4

1.8 litres/3 pints/7½ cups pork and chicken broth, see page 22

120ml/4fl oz/½ cup Sichuan chilli paste, see page 29

4 tbsp Japanese sesame paste (neri goma) or tahini

2 tbsp chilli oil, see page 29

4 portions ramen noodles, see page 38

CHILLI BRAISED RIBS

1kg/2lb 4oz thick pork ribs

1 tbsp crushed small dried red Asian chillies

2 tbsp grated ginger

300ml/10½fl oz/12¼ cups blonde lager

3 garlic cloves, crushed

salt

TOPPING

4 fresh or tinned baby corn, halved lengthways

200g/7oz Chinese broccoli (gai lan)

1 small bunch of coriander

1 batch deep-fried shallots, see page 48

2 tsp Japanese spice mix (shichimi togarashi), see page 48

1. Preheat the oven to 130°C/250°C/Gas 1.

2. Rub the ribs with the chilli, ginger and salt.

3. Place in a deep, ovenproof dish. Pour the lager over the meat and add the garlic cloves. Cover with aluminium foil and roast in the middle of the oven for approximately 4 hours.

4. Bring a large pan of salted water to the boil.

5. Warm the broth in a separate pan.

6. Fill four bowls with hot water to warm them. Discard the water when it's time to plate up.

7. Heat a little vegetable oil in a frying pan and fry the corn until just coloured on the outside, then remove from the pan.

8. Slice the meat and fry the slices in the frying pan until the surface gets crispy and coloured.

9. Blanch the broccoli in the pan of boiling water for 30 seconds. Remove with a sieve and place in cold water, then drain and set aside.

10. Whisk the hot broth together with 2 tbsp Sichuan chilli paste, 1 tbsp sesame paste and ½ tbsp chilli oil in each bowl.

11. Boil the noodles for approximately 45 seconds in the pan of water on a rolling boil. It's best to use a noodle basket or a sieve so that you can reuse the water and quickly take out the noodles once done. You only have a window of a few seconds to make sure they're not under- or overcooked. Drain thoroughly and transfer the noodles to the broth bowls.

12. Top with the meat, broccoli, corn and coriander and sprinkle the deep-fried shallots and spice mix on top.

CHICKEN KATZU RAMEN

Chicken katzu is Japan's answer to the wiener schnitzel. A thick slice of chicken fillet, deep fried until golden with help from super-crunchy panko – the ultimate breadcrumb – that never fails to give a crispy surface. Topping a broth with crispy batter can seem a bit odd since the batter will of course go a little soft once it touches the broth, but it actually works really well. You often see deep-fried food on top of broth bowls in Japan, especially udon noodle dishes, which are traditionally served with deep-fried tempura prawns on top.

SERVES 4

1.6 litres/2¾ pints/6⅔ cups chicken broth,
    see page 25
4–6 tbsp Japanese soy sauce
2 tbsp rice vinegar
4 portions ramen noodles, see page 38
salt

CHICKEN KATZU

2 chicken fillets
115g/4oz/scant ½ cup plain flour
3 eggs, beaten
80g/2¾oz/1½ cups panko breadcrumbs
1–2 litres/1¾–2½pints/4⅓–8 cups oil for
    deep frying

TOPPING

250g/9oz Chinese broccoli (gai lan)
4 spring onions, finely shredded
2 soy sauce pickled eggs, see page 42

1. Halve the chicken fillets lengthways so that you end up with two thin fillets. Sprinkle with salt.

2. Heat up the broth in a pan.

3. Bring a large pan of salted water to the boil for the noodles.

4. Fill four bowls with hot water to warm them. Discard the water when it's time to plate up.

5. Coat the chicken in the flour, then in the egg and finally in the panko. Make sure the panko is covering the meat completely.

6. Heat the oil to 180°C/350°F. Deep fry the chicken fillets for 3–4 minutes until golden brown and crispy (the halved chicken fillets will be thin enough to get cooked through in the hot oil). Remove from the pan and drain on kitchen paper.

7. Mix the broth with 1–1½ tbsp soy sauce and ½ tbsp vinegar in each bowl.

8. Boil the noodles for approximately 45 seconds in the pan of water on a rolling boil. It's best to use a noodle basket or a sieve so that you can reuse the water and quickly take out the noodles once done. You only have a window of a few seconds to make sure they're not under- or overcooked. Drain thoroughly and transfer the noodles to the broth bowls.

9. Top with the fried chicken, broccoli, spring onion and egg halves.

WANTANMEN

Wantan or wonton are filled dumplings that can be served in a broth or deep fried. The dough is more similar to a pasta dough than a gyoza dough. And the actual craft of folding up the parcels is much simpler than gyoza. You simply pinch the dough and filling into a mini bag. The filling varies. I like serving them in a simple soy sauce-flavoured chicken broth and filling with pork and prawns, almost surf 'n' turf style.

SERVES 4

1.6 litres/2¾ pints/6⅔ cups chicken broth, see page 25

6 tbsp Japanese soy sauce

4 tsp white wine vinegar

4 portions ramen noodles, see page 38

WONTONS

150g/5½oz frozen wonton wrappers

2 tbsp vegetable oil

2 spring onions, finely shredded

150g/5½oz raw red prawns or scampi, peeled

150g/5½oz minced pork

1 tbsp finely grated ginger

½ garlic clove, finely grated

1 tsp sesame oil

½ tsp salt

TOPPING

4 spring onions, finely shredded

4 tsp furikake, see page 48

toasted sesame seeds, preferably black and white

1. Defrost the wonton wrappers overnight or leave at room temperature for a few hours.

2. Place the shredded spring onions for the topping in ice-cold water so that they get crunchy and curl up at the edges; they will look *and* taste nice.

3. Heat the oil in a frying pan and sweat the 2 spring onions for the wontons until completely softened.

4. Finely chop the prawns into a mince. Mix together with the pork mince, spring onion, ginger, garlic, sesame oil and salt.

5. Take approximately 1 tbsp of the filling and place in the middle of a wrapper. Dip your finger in cold water and moisten the edges of the wrapper. Press together into a small parcel until the dough is glued together. Repeat to fill the other wrappers.

6. Heat up the broth in a pan. Bring a large pan of salted water to the boil for the noodles.

7. Fill four bowls with hot water to warm them. Discard the water when it's time to plate up.

8. Boil the wonton parcels for about 1½ minutes in the boiling water. Remove with a skimmer.

9. Mix the broth together with 1½ tbsp soy sauce and 1 tsp vinegar in each bowl. Add the wonton parcels.

10. Boil the noodles for approximately 45 seconds in the pan of water on a rolling boil. It's best to use a noodle basket or a sieve so that you can quickly take out the noodles once done. You only have a window of a few seconds to make sure they're not under- or overcooked. Drain thoroughly and transfer the noodles to the broth bowls.

11. Top with the spring onion, furikake and toasted sesame seeds.

BLACK COD RAMEN

The first time I ate black cod it was a revelation: perfectly cooked so that it was flaky on the inside while the outside was completely black with a chargrilled flavour. The cod is marinated in a sweet-sour miso marinade and baked carefully so that it's not overcooked. You then fry the fish quickly in a really hot frying pan so that the surface caramelises. You need 1–2 days to prepare the cod. Here I've used standard cod rather than the special variety of black cod, which is very difficult to source.

SERVES 4

1.8 litres/3 pints/7½ cups pork and chicken broth, see page 22

6 tbsp white miso

4 tsp bonito salt, see page 31

2 tbsp freshly squeezed lemon juice

4 portions ramen noodles, see page 38

BLACK COD

500g/1lb 2oz fresh cod fillet without skin, in four pieces

50ml/1¾fl oz/3 tbsp sake

50ml/1¾fl oz/3 tbsp mirin

100ml/3½fl oz/scant ½ cup white miso

40g/1½oz/¼ cup granulated sugar

TOPPING

20g/¾oz shredded, dried mushroom (black fungus)

2 soy sauce pickled eggs, see page 42

4 spring onions, finely shredded

80g/2¾oz mizuna leaves or spinach

1. One or two days in advance, prepare the cod. Bring the sake and mirin to the boil. Remove from the heat and whisk in the miso. Reheat and add the sugar. Leave on the heat until the sugar has melted. Leave to cool and place the marinade and fish in a bag. Marinate for 1–2 days in the fridge.

2. At the time of serving, heat the broth in a pan.

3. Bring a large pan of salted water to the boil.

4. Fill four bowls with hot water to warm them. Discard the water when it's time to plate up.

5. Soak the mushrooms in boiling hot salted water for 20 minutes.

6. Heat up a frying pan, preferably non-stick so that the fish doesn't stick (the marinade is very sweet and burns easily in a cast-iron pan).

7. Add some oil and fry the fish for about 2 minutes on each side. The pan should be hot so the crust caramelises and blackens.

8. Whisk together the broth and 1½ tbsp miso in each bowl. Add bonito salt to taste. Squeeze in the lemon to freshen up the broth. The acidity together with the saltiness and the slightly sweet fish is a great combination.

9. Boil the noodles for approximately 45 seconds in the pan of water on a rolling boil. It's best to use a noodle basket or a sieve so that you can quickly take out the noodles once done. You only have a window of a few seconds to make sure they're not under- or overcooked. Drain thoroughly and transfer the noodles to the broth bowls.

10. Top with the fish, mushrooms, egg halves, spring onion and mizuna.

Corn 'n' crab ramen and
lemon clam ramen

CORN'N'CRAB RAMEN

Citrusy chicken broth topped with king crab and crunchy daikon. If yuzu is in season you can squeeze some into the broth as well. If not, standard lemon or tinned yuzu will do. If you can't find mizuna leaves in the supermarket (they can be quite difficult to find), you can use spinach or coriander.

SERVES 4

1.8 litres/3 pints/7½ cups chicken broth, see page 25, or 1.8 litres/3 pints/7½ cups dashi broth, see page 22

4 tbsp freshly squeezed lemon or yuzu juice

sea salt

4 portions ramen noodles, see page 38

TOPPING

2–3 legs from king crabs with shell, approximately 400g/14oz total weight

150g/5½oz fresh watermelon radish or daikon, finely shredded

1 fresh corn on the cob, sliced

4 spring onions, finely shredded

2 soy sauce pickled eggs, see page 42

80g/2¾oz mizuna leaves or spinach or coriander

1. Pick the crab meat. Heat up the broth in a pan. Add half of the crab shells and leave to simmer for approximately 15 minutes. Remove the shells.

2. Place the shredded radish or daikon in ice-cold water for at least 15 minutes so that it goes really crunchy.

3. Bring a large pan of salted water to the boil for the noodles.

4. Fill four bowls with hot water to warm them. Discard the water when it's time to plate up.

5. Boil the sweetcorn for approximately 2 minutes in the pan of boiling water and remove with a sieve.

6. Add lemon juice and salt to the broth to taste. Ladle the broth into the bowls.

7. Boil the noodles for approximately 45 seconds in the pan of water on a rolling boil. It's best to use a noodle basket or a sieve so that you can reuse the water and quickly take out the noodles once done. You only have a window of a few seconds to make sure they're not under- or overcooked. Drain thoroughly and transfer the noodles to the broth bowls.

8. Top with the crab, radish, corn, spring onion, egg halves and mizuna.

LEMON CLAM RAMEN

Cooking a ramen broth from clams isn't that unusual. Often pork or chicken broth is mixed with the shellfish to add some weight and complexity to the flavour. You can serve ramen with small clams such as cockles or palourde clams, but there are also broths made from giant clams – these are larger than blue mussels and sometimes as big as 20 centimetres! They add an enormous amount of flavour to the broth and are used for more delicate ramen. For this recipe you can either use chicken broth or make the quick version from water and clams. In both cases it can be nice to flavour the broth with some chicken fat if you happen to have any in the fridge.

SERVES 4

1kg/2lb 4oz cockles or clams

salt

2 garlic cloves, peeled

1.8 litres/3 pints/7½ cups water or chicken broth,
    see page 25

1 piece of kombu seaweed (approximately 3–4g)

2–4 tsp bonito salt, see page 31

2 tbsp chicken fat, see page 28 (optional)

4 portions ramen noodles, see page 38

TOPPING

4 roasted tomatoes, see page 47

4 spring onions, finely shredded

1 lemon, finely sliced

freshly ground black pepper

1. Place the clams in cold water in a bucket. Salt the water so that it's as salty as seawater. Leave to stand for 1–2 hours in the fridge. If the clams contain a lot of sand they will spit it out into the water.

2. Rinse the clams and discard any that are broken or don't close up.

3. Bring a large pan of salted water to the boil for the noodles.

4. Fill four bowls with hot water to warm them. Discard the water when it's time to plate up.

5. Bring the water or chicken broth to the boil in a pan. Add the garlic and kombu and simmer for 10 minutes.

6. Add the clams and boil for 2 minutes until they have opened. Remove the boiled garlic and the kombu. Add the bonito salt to the broth to taste and stir in the chicken fat, if using. Ladle the broth into the bowls. Save the clams in the pan.

7. Boil the noodles for approximately 45 seconds in the pan of water on a rolling boil. It's best to use a noodle basket or a sieve so that you can reuse the water and quickly take out the noodles once done. You only have a window of a few seconds to make sure they're not under- or overcooked. Drain thoroughly and transfer the noodles to the broth bowls.

8. Top with the clams, tomato, spring onion and lemon slices and sprinkle over freshly ground black pepper.

INSTANT RAMEN

FOR A RAMEN ADDICT, THE CRAVING CAN SET IN AT ANY TIME, and when it does you just *have* to have a bowl of salty broth and boiled noodles. The long cooking time that is a prerequisite for a really good broth complicates things a little. If you're prepared and have broth and noodles in the freezer, you'll have it ready in minutes, but it's the advance work that takes the time, so make sure you've always got the freezer stocked up!

You might not always have time to cook broth, even in advance. There are a few shortcuts: dashi, mushroom, veggie and chicken broth can actually be cooked fairly quickly. The resulting flavour isn't quite as complex but if you season the broth properly with salt and tare it will still taste great. The chicken broth will need to boil for at least an hour to allow the fat to melt into the liquid, although the tasty gelatinous qualities won't have had time to fully develop yet. Mushroom and dashi broths shouldn't boil for too long, but instead sit to infuse – one to two hours is usually enough. And then we've got the magic miso. With miso you can get amazing flavours – just add it to the broth for saltiness, umami and extra punch.

And what about the noodles? There are some shop-bought noodles that are perfectly okay. I like the semi-fresh vacuum-packed ones that you find in Asian food shops the best. They sometimes pull off that texture you're after, the noodles sticking together in the fatty broth. The dried ones often don't contain enough starch and won't absorb the broth in the same way. You have to shop around to find your favourite.

Where I live it's a bit difficult to find fresh noodles in the supermarkets. But if you ever visit the US you'll feel both jealous and happy walking around a standard supermarket and looking at the choice of noodles available. I have for several years stuffed my suitcase full of fresh Sun Noodles any time I visit the US. These are made with good-quality flour and genuine kansui that gives them that 'chewy' bounce, and they are jam-packed with starch, which means the broth gets soaked up and sticks to the noodles. Sun Noodles have gained praise over the last few years and the best ramen places in the US – Momofuku, Ivan Ramen, Ramen-Shop, Bassanova – all serve them. Now the company has opened a ramen lab in New York where they experiment with broths and noodles, and invite ramen chefs for guest performances.

You can understand why instant ramen became such a success when it launched in the 50s. In only 3 minutes, you could get a steaming bowl of ramen that was packed with saltiness and flavour. Momofuku Ando, the namesake of chef David Chang's renowned ramen bar in New York, founded Nissin Food in Japan in 1958 and launched the product Chikin Ramen. An instant ramen in a small pack with parboiled deep-fried noodles that could be rehydrated extremely quickly in hot water together with concentrated broth. At the beginning of the 70s, Cup Noodles were introduced with enormous success and today you can find them in each and every shop in the US. When the dried instant noodles turned up on the Swedish shop shelves in the 90s, I was one of those who stocked up on the square packets and ate them for lunch, often flavoured with curry powder, and with some added chopped vegetables. When the genuine slow-cooked ramen came into my life I was completely hooked.

COLD DASHI RAMEN

A perfect summer dish. The dashi broth is served chilled with ice cubes to allow you to cool down in the heat, and is flavoured with lemon juice, which gives it a fresh acidity. Shiso is a type of cress that can be a bit tricky to source, but you can grow it yourself if you're green fingered. If you can't find it you can use Thai basil or coriander instead to add some fragrance to the dish.

SERVES 4

1.6 litres/2¾ pints/6⅔ cups dashi broth, see page 22

4 portions ramen noodles, see page 38

juice of ½ lemon

150ml/5fl oz/scant ⅔ cup crushed ice

salt

TOPPING

4 roasted tomatoes, see page 47

300g/10½oz meat from king crab (1–2 legs)

1 pack shiso leaves

3 spring onions, finely shredded

1 lemon, finely sliced

1. Warm up the dashi broth in a pan until tepid. Season to taste with salt. Leave to cool.

2. Bring a large pan of salted water to the boil for the noodles.

3. Boil the noodles for approximately 45 seconds in the pan of water on a rolling boil. It's best to use a noodle basket or a sieve so that you can reuse the water and quickly take out the noodles once done. You only have a window of a few seconds to make sure they're not under- or overcooked. Drain thoroughly and place in ice-cold water, preferably with added ice.

4. Mix the dashi broth with the lemon juice and ladle into four bowls.

5. Add the cold noodles to the broth bowls and add the crushed ice.

6. Top with the roasted tomato, crab, shiso and spring onion. Place lemon slices along the edge of the bowl. Serve immediately before the ice melts.

003
OTHER JAPANESE
NOODLES

It's impossible to resist including a few recipes for tsukemen, udon and soba noodles in a book about ramen. Tsukemen (skemen) are cold, often slightly thicker, ramen noodles served with a hot, concentrated broth on the side for dipping. Many ramen bars serve both ramen and tsukemen. Udon and soba noodles are eaten both hot and cold. According to Japanese tradition you eat them hot in a dashi broth or cold with a dipping sauce made from soy sauce, grated daikon and spring onion. Tempura is often served with udon noodles.

SICHUAN TSUKEMEN

At many ramen places specialising in hot and spicy kotteri ramen you can order different heat levels for your broth, since Sichuan pepper has a numbing effect in the mouth. Lunch guests sit at the bar, sniffling and sweating over the hot and spicy broth. My favourite recipe is served at Kikanbo in Tokyo. The Sichuan pepper mixed together with the thick broth is one of the best things you can eat in the world of ramen. Thick, plump, peppery, deep and hot. Either you serve just noodles and the basic broth for tsukemen or you can also add some kind of meat or chicken to the dish. There are several ways to do this: sometimes the meat is added to the hot broth, sometimes it's served on the side on a separate plate, and other times it's presented next to the cold noodles on the same plate.

SERVES 4

8 tbsp Sichuan chilli paste, see page 29

900ml/1½ pints/3¾ cups tonkotsu broth or
chicken broth, see page 25

3 tsp cornflour

1½ tbsp cold water

4 portions ramen noodles, see page 38

salt

TOPPING

4 tbsp chopped nori seaweed

20g/¾oz coriander, coarsely chopped

4 spring onions, finely shredded

4 tbsp bonito flakes (katsuobushi)

1. Bring a large pan of salted water to the boil.

2. Sweat the chilli paste for approximately 1 minute in a wok or casserole dish. Add the broth and bring to the boil.

3. Mix the cornflour with the cold water and whisk into the broth. Simmer gently for 10 minutes, until the broth has thickened a little.

4. Boil the noodles for approximately 45 seconds in the pan of water on a rolling boil. It's best to use a noodle basket or a sieve so that you can reuse the water and quickly take out the noodles once done. You only have a window of a few seconds to make sure they're not under- or overcooked. Drain and place in ice-cold water. Change the water if the noodles don't cool down fully.

5. Place the noodles on a serving plate and top with the nori seaweed.

6. Ladle the broth into bowls or serve directly from the wok if everyone can dip into the same bowl.

7. Top the broth with the coriander, spring onion and bonito flakes.

～～～～～～～～～～

COLD NOODLES AND HOT BROTH

Some ramen joints focus solely on cold noodles and hot broth. If you eat slowly it can happen that the broth gets cold. Some places have hot stones that you can place in the bowl to heat it up again. When you've finished dipping your noodles you fill the bowl with hot water to dilute the concentrated broth left at the bottom so that you can drink the rest directly from the bowl.

BEEF BROTH TSUKEMEN

Rich hot broth for cold noodles. At many tsukemen places they serve a broth cooked from dried fish and garnished with fish salt. Sometimes it tastes great, sometimes quite 'funky'. A favourite is Fuunji in Tokyo. There they make a pork and chicken broth with dried mackerel garnished with fish salt. It's an acquired taste! For my beef broth tsukemen I use a broth made from beef, flavoured with miso, shrimp paste and soy sauce and topped with fish salt made from bonito. If you haven't still got the meat from when you boiled the broth you can add some pork mince or chicken, or just omit the meat.

SERVES 4

200g/7oz oxtail meat (from the broth)

1 tbsp vegetable oil

900ml/1½ pints/3¾ cups beef bone broth, see page 26

3 tsp cornflour

2 tbsp cold water

2 tbsp red miso paste

2 tbsp shrimp paste (optional)

2 tbsp rice vinegar

1½ tbsp Chinese soy sauce

4 portions ramen noodles, see page 38

TOPPING

1½ tbsp shredded, dried mushrooms (black fungus)

4 lime slices

4 soy sauce pickled egg yolks, see page 47

3 spring onions, finely shredded

4 tbsp pickled ginger (gari), see page 144

2 tsp bonito salt, see page 31

1. Bring a large pan of salted water to the boil for the noodles.

2. Pick off the meat from the oxtail.

3. Bring another pan of salted water to the boil and add the dried mushrooms. Leave to soak for approximately 20 minutes.

4. Heat the oil in a pan and quickly sweat the oxtail, then add the broth and bring to the boil.

5. Whisk together the cornflour and cold water. Stir into the broth, a little at a time and simmer until the broth thickens. Whisk in the miso, shrimp paste, vinegar and soy sauce.

6. Boil the noodles for approximately 45 seconds in the pan of water on a rolling boil. It's best to use a noodle basket or a sieve so that you can reuse the water and quickly take out the noodles once done. You only have a window of a few seconds to make sure they're not under- or overcooked. Drain thoroughly and rinse in cold water. Place in a bowl with ice-cold water and make sure that the noodles get cold and springy.

7. Ladle the broth and meat into bowls. Top with the mushrooms, lime slices, pickled egg yolks, spring onion, pickled ginger and a pinch of bonito salt. Serve with the cold noodles on the side.

BBQ YUZU TSUKEMEN

The noodles have a nice chewiness and springiness when they're cold and they are heated to just the right temperature by the hot broth which sticks to them. Super delicious. Yuzu is fragrant and fresh at the same time. Unfortunately, fresh yuzu has a very short season and is difficult to get hold of in standard supermarkets, but you can find decent yuzu juice in a bottle or can in Asian food shops. It's fine for adding to broths and dressings but you won't get the extra flavour from the zest.

SERVES 4

2 tbsp Japanese spice mix (shichimi togarashi), see page 48

900ml/1½ pints/3¾ cups tonkotsu broth, see page 25

1 tbsp garlic purée, see page 30

4 tbsp Japanese sesame paste (neri goma) or tahini

1½ tbsp finely grated ginger root

4 tbsp Japanese soy sauce

4 portions thicker ramen noodles, see page 38

freshly squeezed juice of 1 yuzu or 3 tbsp yuzu juice

vegetable oil

TOPPING

400g/14oz BBQ pork, see page 46

150g/5½oz fresh beansprouts

4 lemon slices

4 spring onions, finely sliced

4 soy sauce pickled eggs, see page 42

40g/1½oz/scant 1 cup chopped coriander

finely shredded zest of 1 yuzu or 1 lemon

vegetable oil

1. Slice up the BBQ pork and place on a baking tray.

2. Bring a large pan of salted water to the boil for the noodles.

3. Heat up a wok or a sauté pan until it's really hot. Fry the beansprouts quickly over a high heat so that they become slightly charred. Remove from the heat and set aside.

4. Heat up a little oil in the wok. Add the spice mix and fry for 30 seconds. Add the broth, garlic purée, sesame paste, ginger and soy sauce. Bring to the boil and keep hot.

5. Boil the noodles for approximately 45 seconds in the pan of water on a rolling boil. It's best to use a noodle basket or a sieve so that you can reuse the water and quickly take out the noodles once done. You only have a window of a few seconds to make sure they're not under- or overcooked. Rinse the noodles in cold water and transfer to a bowl filled with ice-cold water.

6. Drain the noodles and divide between four plates. Top with the beansprouts, a lemon slice and the spring onion.

7. Mix the yuzu juice into the broth and ladle the broth into bowls.

8. Top with the meat, egg, coriander and yuzu zest.

9. Serve the broth piping hot and dip the cold noodles into it.

Tsukemen at Kikanbo in Chiyoda, Tokyo. Pictured are the thick broth and the charred beansprouts that top the tsukemen noodles.

UDON WITH SESAME DIP

Ice-cold chewy udon noodles that are dipped into a cold thick sesame sauce. This is a favourite. Every time I visit London I go to the Japanese noodle bar Koya and order tempura, udon and the delicious sesame sauce. I actually prefer udon with a cold dip instead of hot dashi broth: I think the texture of the noodles comes into its own when they are served cold.

SERVES 4

1 batch udon noodles, see page 39

4 tbsp finely shredded nori seaweed

SESAME DIP

100ml/3½fl oz/scant ½ cup Japanese sesame
    paste (neri goma) or tahini

1 tbsp white miso paste

3 tbsp cold water

1 tbsp finely grated ginger

2½ tbsp rice vinegar

2 tbsp Japanese soy sauce

2 tbsp toasted sesame seeds, crushed

4 spring onions, finely shredded

1. Bring a large pan of salted water to the boil.

2. Whisk together the sesame paste, miso, cold water, ginger, vinegar and soy sauce to make a dipping sauce. Keep cool until serving.

3. Prepare a large bowl with ice-cold water.

4. Boil the noodles in the pan of water on a rolling boil for approximately 2 minutes. They are usually done when they float up to the surface.

5. Take out the noodles with a sieve or drain in a colander. Place in the ice-cold water so that the noodles cool down and retain their tasty chewy texture.

6. Fold the toasted sesame seeds into the sauce and garnish with spring onion.

7. Serve the cold noodles topped with nori seaweed and with the dipping sauce on the side.

UDON WITH TEMPURA

Tempura and udon is a classic combination. You can recognise the sound at udon places when the crispy deep-fried tempura hits the dashi broth just before serving. The udon noodles are served warm in a simple dashi broth flavoured with soy sauce and daikon. On top sits a crispy prawn and some chopped spring onion. You need to grab the prawn straightaway to savour its crispiness before it disappears into the broth. The dish also often comes topped with deep-fried pieces of tempura batter, almost like croutons. You cook these before you fry the prawns by dripping tempura batter into the hot oil and deep frying until crispy. If you try this at home, take out the batter bits with a skimmer and drain quickly on kitchen paper before serving.

SERVES 4

1.6 litres/2¾ pints/6⅔ cups dashi broth,
    see page 22

2 tsp finely grated fresh daikon

6 tbsp Japanese soy sauce

1 batch udon noodles, see page 39

4 spring onions, finely shredded

PRAWN TEMPURA

8 fresh raw red prawns

2 litres/3½ pints/8 cups oil for deep frying

tempura batter, see page 129

1. Bring a large pan of salted water to the boil for the noodles.

2. Fill four bowls with hot water to warm them up. Discard the water when it's time to plate up.

3. Heat the broth in a pan.

4. Peel the prawns if you wish (you can leave them in their shells if you prefer), but leave the tails on.

5. Heat the oil ready for deep frying.

6. Whisk together the tempura batter.

7. Dip the prawns into the batter, lift out and deep fry for approximately 1 minute until crispy. Remove and drain on kitchen paper.

8. Divide the daikon and soy sauce between the four bowls and mix in the broth.

9. Boil the noodles in the pan of water on a rolling boil for approximately 2 minutes. Drain and add to the broth bowls.

10. Top with the spring onion and freshly fried prawns.

BREAKFAST UDON

A British take on udon. A little bit like a full English breakfast but with noodles instead of baked beans. Traditionally udon is eaten for breakfast or lunch in Japan and many udon places close for the evening, when ramen takes over. The udon masters make the dough early in the morning, and the queues outside the best udon places are there all morning.

SERVES 4

1.2 litres/2 pints/5 cups dashi broth, see page 22

1 batch udon noodles, see page 39

salt

TOPPING

140g/14oz bacon

4 eggs

4 roasted tomatoes, see page 47

1 batch deep-fried shallots, see page 48

oil for frying

1. Bring a large pan of salted water to the boil for the noodles.

2. Fill four bowls with hot water to warm them up. Discard the water when it's time to plate up.

3. Fry the bacon in a little oil until crispy

4. Fry the eggs in some oil until crispy underneath, 'sunny side up'.

5. Heat the broth in a pan, season with salt and ladle into the four bowls.

6. Boil the noodles in the pan of water on a rolling boil for approximately 2 minutes. Drain and transfer the noodles to the broth bowls.

7. Top with the bacon, egg, tomato and deep-fried shallots. Serve steaming hot.

SOBA, SOY SAUCE & DAIKON

Soba noodles can be served both hot and cold. In the winter time they are mostly paired with a hot broth made from dashi and soy sauce, and they are served either in the broth or cold on the side, as they will get dipped into the hot broth anyway. In the summer time they are mostly served cold with just a little bit of soy sauce, daikon and spring onion.

SERVES 4

1 batch soba noodles, see page 39

200ml/7fl oz/scant 1 cup Japanese soy sauce

4 spring onions, finely shredded

20cm/8in fresh daikon, peeled and finely grated

1. Boil the noodles in a large pan of salted water for no more than 60 seconds.

2. Drain and cool them down in ice-cold water, preferably with added ice.

3. Drain again and transfer to a serving plate.

4. Serve with the soy sauce, spring onion and daikon.

SPECIALISED SOBA RESTAURANTS

I've been at soba restaurants where they serve at least 15 courses of different buckwheat dishes. You even drink buckwheat water and shochu, a spirit made from buckwheat. It's tasty and interesting, but after I've left I've often felt that I can do without buckwheat for a few weeks! What surprises me the most is that the buckwheat noodles, the star of the show, aren't served until the very end. And when they are, they will come in two different courses so that you first get soba noodles made from slightly less 'fancy' buckwheat, and after that the most exclusive noodles, shin soba, made from buckwheat that's homegrown by the master and ground just before it's made into dough. These are packed with buckwheat flavour, almost with a hint of nuttiness. Soba noodles are made solely from buckwheat which is, by and large, something that only a soba master can do. It's incredibly difficult to do since there is no gluten in the flour to bind the dough together and make it supple. To make soba at home, therefore, I use both buckwheat and wheat flour in the dough (see page 39).

004
SMALL
PLATES

Side dishes are one of Japanese cuisine's highlights. Gyoza and pickles are sometimes served with your ramen even though they, just like all the other recipes in this chapter, can just as well be eaten on their own as a snack. Pictured below is a yakitori place in Piss Alley, also called Memory Lane, behind Shinjuku station. In small, narrow spaces you're greeted by smoke clouds and clinking, well-filled beer glasses mixed with the mouthwatering aroma of grilled yakitori.

FRIED CHICKEN

Nagoya tebasaki – the Japanese version of fried chicken. When you bite through the crispy crust and taste the flavour-rich, succulent chicken you just want more. The meat is marinated for up to two days before it's deep fried. I make the marinade similar to buttermilk fried chicken, with soured cream that tenderises and adds a stickiness that finds its way into the meat.

SERVES 4

- 1kg/2lb 4oz chicken, preferably thighs, drumsticks and wings
- 2 litres/3½ pints/8 cups oil for deep frying

MARINADE

- 200ml/7fl oz/scant 1 cup soured cream
- 3 tbsp Japanese soy sauce
- 2 tbsp white miso paste
- 2 tbsp finely grated ginger
- 1 garlic clove, finely grated
- 2 tbsp rice vinegar
- 2 tbsp Korean chilli powder (gochugaru)
- 1½ tsp salt

BATTER

- 175g/6oz/1⅓ cups plain flour
- 90g/3oz/scant 1 cup cornflour
- 1 tbsp baking powder
- 1½ tsp salt
- 3 eggs
- 2 tbsp water

SAUCE

- 3 tbsp Japanese soy sauce
- 2 tbsp mirin
- 2 tbsp water
- 3 tbsp Korean chilli paste (gochujang)
- 2 tbsp rice vinegar
- 1 tsp sesame oil
- ½ garlic clove, peeled
- 1 tbsp finely chopped ginger
- 1½ tbsp toasted sesame seeds, preferably black and white

1. One to two days in advance: mix together all the ingredients for the marinade and place the chicken and marinade in a resealable plastic food bag. Leave to marinate in the fridge for 1–2 days.

2. Before serving, simmer all the sauce ingredients together, apart from the sesame seeds, for about 5 minutes. Remove from the heat and blend until smooth. Add the sesame seeds and give another whizz, the seeds should still be almost whole.

3. Heat the oil to 170°C/320°F in a pan or fryer.

4. Mix the flours, baking powder and salt in a bowl. In a separate bowl, whisk the egg and water together.

5. Take out the chicken and roll in the flour until all the chicken pieces are completely covered. Dip the chicken into the egg, and then into the flour again.

6. Deep fry the pieces in batches for 10–12 minutes until they're cooked through and golden brown. Turn the pieces over every other minute.

7. Remove with a skimmer. Drain on kitchen paper.

8. Drizzle over the sauce just before serving.

Crispy prawn daikon, tofu with sesame, cucumber with miso, sweetcorn with ponzu, sesame-fried spinach and pumpkin cooked in dashi.

SWEETCORN WITH PONZU

Grilled sweetcorn with a salty-sour ponzu dressing and shiso leaves. Shiso can be difficult to find, but can be replaced by Thai basil, which also has a fragrant flavour.

SERVES 4

2 fresh corn on the cob, or 180g/6½oz/
    scant 1⅓ cups frozen sweetcorn kernels

2 tbsp vegetable oil

3 tbsp water

3 lemon slices

1 batch ponzu, see page 136

20g/¾oz shiso or Thai basil

salt

1. Cut the corn off the cob. If you have a grill you can first grill the cobs and then cut the corn off.
2. Heat the oil in a frying pan and fry the sweetcorn. Add the water after 1 minute and leave to cook so that the water is absorbed by the corn. Add salt and leave the corn in the pan until coloured. Transfer to a serving plate together with the lemon slices.
3. Pour over the ponzu dressing and top with shiso.

TOFU WITH SESAME

There are different kinds of tofu: firm, smoked, soft and silken. My favourite is silken tofu: it can be served in a soup, deep fried in tempura batter, panko or flour, or like here, sliced and served cold with a dressing. If you want to vary the dish you can coat the tofu in a mixture of plain flour and cornflour, then deep fry it until crispy and serve topped with the dressing.

SERVES 4

3 tbsp Japanese soy sauce

1 tbsp mirin

1 tsp sesame oil

1 tbsp dried bonito flakes (katsuobushi)

2 tsp finely grated ginger root

1 tbsp rapeseed oil with a neutral flavour

1½ tbsp toasted sesame seeds, preferably black
    and white

300g/10½oz silken tofu

1. Mix the soy sauce, mirin, sesame oil, bonito flakes, ginger and rapeseed oil to make a dressing.
2. Add the sesame seeds.
3. Slice up the tofu and place on a plate. Drizzle over the dressing.

SESAME-FRIED SPINACH

In Asian food shops you can sometimes find water spinach with more stalk and bitterness than standard spinach. If unavailable, you can replace it with chard or standard spinach.

SERVES 4

3 tbsp vegetable oil

2 garlic cloves, finely sliced

2 tsp sesame oil

200g/7oz water spinach, chard or spinach

3 tbsp water

salt

1. Heat the vegetable oil in a frying pan over a medium heat and deep fry the garlic until golden brown. Transfer to a plate.
2. Heat up the pan again and add the sesame oil.
3. Add the spinach and water. Let the water absorb into the spinach over a high heat. Add salt. Stir in the fried garlic and serve.

CRISPY PRAWN DAIKON

Crunchy daikon with a crispy hash made from chopped prawns, chilli and garlic. The prawns should be blended or chopped with the shells still on – the shells add flavour when heated up. Watermelon radish can be difficult to get hold of but standard white daikon works just as well.

SERVES 4

450g/1lb fresh daikon, preferably a mix of white daikon and watermelon radish

8 fresh prawns with shells on

2 tbsp vegetable oil

1 tbsp finely chopped ginger

½ garlic clove, finely chopped

1 tbsp chilli oil, shop bought or homemade, see page 29

1½ tbsp rice vinegar

10g/½oz coriander, leaves only

salt

1. Peel and slice the daikon and radishes thinly using a mandolin. Place in ice-cold water for approximately 10 minutes so that they get crunchy.
2. Remove the heads from the prawns. Blend the prawns with the shell on in a food processor or chop very finely with a knife.
3. Heat the vegetable oil in a frying pan and sauté the prawns and the ginger over a high heat.
4. When the prawns start to crisp up, lower the heat and add the garlic and chilli oil. Fry for another minute. Remove from the heat and season with salt.
5. Drain the daikon and radishes and leave to drain on kitchen paper, then toss with the vinegar in a bowl.
6. Serve the daikon and radishes topped with the crispy prawns and coriander.

ONSEN EGG WITH DASHI

This is a classic Japanese way of serving onsen eggs, the soft-boiled eggs that simmer slowly in 63–65 °C water until both white and yolk have almost the same texture. Usually the egg is served in a dashi broth; here it's topped with spring onion and furikake.

SERVES 4

> 400ml/14fl oz/1²/₃ cups dashi broth, see page 22
>
> 4 x 64-degree eggs, see page 46
>
> 2 spring onions, finely shredded
>
> 4 tsp furikake, see page 48
>
> salt

1. Heat up the broth. Season to taste with salt.
2. Ladle into four small bowls and crack in an egg. Sprinkle with spring onion and furikake.

CUCUMBER WITH MISO

Crispy cucumber with a salty, creamy miso dressing. This dish works best with cold cucumber.

SERVES 4

> 3 tbsp miso paste
>
> 1 tbsp cold water
>
> 1½ tbsp rice vinegar
>
> ½ tbsp Japanese soy sauce
>
> 1 tsp finely grated ginger
>
> 1 cucumber
>
> 1 tbsp toasted sesame seeds

1. Whisk the miso, water, vinegar, soy sauce and ginger together.
2. Cut the cucumber into chunks, and top with the miso dressing and sesame seeds.

PUMPKIN COOKED IN DASHI

Boiling vegetables, tofu, egg and meat in dashi is an old tradition in Japan. The ingredients get a nice deep flavour from the seaweed and dried bonito. Slow cooking in dashi is called oden, and when you go into a 7-Eleven in Japan you might wonder what it is you can smell. That's oden. At the till they have simmering oden that you can pick up as fast food on the go, a little bit like a salad bar but with cooked food.

SERVES 4

> 1 litre/38fl oz/4²/₃ cups dashi broth, see page 22
>
> 400g/14oz pumpkin, for example delicata or
>   hokkaido squash
>
> 1 tbsp furikake, see page 48
>
> salt

1. Heat up the broth in a pan that holds approximately 2 litres/3½ pints/8 cups. Season to taste with salt.
2. Peel and remove the seeds from the pumpkin and cut the flesh into dice.
3. Leave the pumpkin to simmer in the broth for approximately 20 minutes, until softened. Serve the pumpkin topped with furikake.

TEMPURA

ADDICTIVELY TASTY. Crunchy, crispy vegetables and seafood are deep fried to perfection in a sizzling hot oil bath. Here, it's all about a good batter, and being quick both when cooking and serving. It's almost a matter of seconds. You can often think that you've failed with your deep frying, but the tempura always softens after a while – it won't hold the crispiness for a long time so needs to be eaten piping hot, straight after being taken out of the oil.

It's a fine art of course, just like with everything else in Japan. To deep fry like the deep-frying masters, it takes many years of experience. They can hear from the sound when it's time to take the tempura out of the hot oil and know exactly what consistency the batter should have. It should be pretty runny and stick around the vegetables and seafood when they're dipped into it, but not coat them too thickly. Never prepare the batter in advance, instead whisk it together just before frying.

You usually deep fry in an oil with neutral flavour, for example rapeseed or vegetable, but some mix the neutral oil with sesame oil for extra flavour. You need to make sure that the oil is hot, somewhere between 170°C and 180°C (320–350°F). No hotter, or the vegetables will get burnt.

You can deep fry most things in tempura batter but most common are vegetables, seafood, chicken and tofu. Broccoli, courgettes, sweet potato, aubergine, pumpkin, carrot, okra, onion, shiitake, enoki, asparagus or peppers are also popular. And the most important thing of all, vegetables and batter should both be cold before being added to the hot oil bath, so that they go properly crispy.

The actual deep frying is pretty easy. You need to make sure that the oil is at the right temperature and don't fry too much in one go, or it will lower the temperature of the oil. Add vegetables, fish, seafood and tofu using tweezers or tongs. Drag them back and forth in the oil a couple of times so that they don't stick to the bottom or fry unevenly. If you make small cuts along the back of a prawn it will go straight and you can also stretch it out with two chopsticks so that it doesn't curl when deep fried. Fry for approximately 1 minute depending on the ingredient. Some vegetables, like thicker chunks of pumpkin, should fry for around 2–3 minutes to get cooked through. Take out with a skimmer and serve directly on a piece of kitchen paper, a rack or waxed paper. Note that the tempura shouldn't be left to drain for long, like you would with onion rings, chips or fried chicken. The tempura should be served immediately, just at the point when you no longer burn your fingers on it. It's best to serve in batches; vegetables first, then perhaps mushrooms, and after that prawns and fish. Your guests will just have to sit down and wait, listening to the deep frying sizzling and crackling away.

The most classic condiment for tempura is a dipping sauce made from soy sauce, mirin, daikon and ginger. You can also serve with a dipping salt. But you can experiment as you wish. If you want to dip your tempura into a hot sauce you can simply mix one together with some chilli, otherwise a salt-sour ponzu made from soy sauce and yuzu is also really good.

TEMPURA

You can pretty much fry whatever you like for your tempura. Remember that thick slices of vegetables and fish need longer in the deep fryer than thin slices of vegetables and mushrooms.

SERVES 4–6

mixed vegetables, seafood, fish and tofu

1–2 litres/3½ pints/8 cups oil for deep frying

160g/5oz plain flour

dipping sauce of your choice and/or dipping salt, see recipes to the right

TEMPURA BATTER

200g/7oz/scant 1 cup plain flour

60g/2oz/scant ⅔ cup cornflour

1 egg yolk

300ml/10½fl oz/1¼ cups ice-cold sparkling water

1. Cut all the vegetables, fish and shellfish into suitably sized chunks. Place in the fridge.

2. Heat the oil to 180°C/350°F.

3. Put the plain flour into a bowl.

4. Make the tempura batter in another bowl: whisk together the flours, egg yolk and water into a smooth batter. Don't whisk to much, or the batter will get chewy from the gluten and won't crisp up when deep frying.

5. Dip the vegetables, fish and shellfish into the flour first and then into the batter. Deep fry in batches.

6. Drain on kitchen paper or waxed paper. Serve immediately together with one or more dipping sauces and dipping salt.

DIPPING SAUCES & SALTS

Dip the hot, crispy, freshly deep-fried tempura into one or more of these dipping sauces or dipping salts.

SOY SAUCE & DAIKON

6 tbsp Japanese soy sauce

2 tbsp mirin

4 tbsp finely grated ginger

4 tsp wasabi

Mix together all the ingredients.

PONZU, SEE PAGE 136

BONITO & SESAME SALT

6g/⅛oz bonito flakes (katsuobushi)

2 tbsp toasted sesame seeds

3 tbsp sea salt

Blend all the ingredients together into a fine salt, or crush using a pestle and mortar.

MATCHA & LEMON SALT

3 tbsp sea salt

½ tbsp matcha powder

finely grated zest of ½ lemon

Blend all the ingredients together into a fine salt, or crush using a pestle and mortar.

GYOZA

There are dumplings, pierogi, wontons, ravioli, tortellini and loads of other forms of dough parcels the world over. Japan's version are gyoza, which were introduced into Japanese cuisine about the same time as ramen, just after the Second World War.

A thin round wheat dough wrapper with quite a lot of starch from cornflour or potato flour is folded around a tasty filling using a special technique. The parcels are both fried and steamed, until they are soft on the top and extremely crispy and golden brown underneath.

The folding technique is an art. You want small pleats on one side of the dough while the other side is completely smooth (see picture) for the authentic look. But you can pinch them together however you like, as long as they stick together during the frying and steaming.

When gyoza are served the right way, they come on a plate with the crispy side facing upwards, the small parcels almost glued together from the starch. Very pretty. This you achieve by placing the parcels really close together in the pan so that they stick together with the starch that is seeping out of the dough and the liquid that you pour into the pan. You can of course fry the parcels separately too if you wish.

I often buy ready-made frozen gyoza dough. It usually has a dusting of white potato flour or cornflour, but sometimes it's completely clean and then it's difficult to get it to stick together with the other parcels in the pan and doesn't get as crispy either, as the starch also contributes to the crispiness.

Gyoza are perfect for freezing and taking out when you get a craving for the crispy little parcels. Make a double batch and dry them separately on clingfilm for about 4 hours. Then place them in a freezer bag. You don't need to defrost them but can fry them immediately – just fry them for a minute or so longer.

GYOZA DOUGH

If you can't find ready-made gyoza dough it's worth making your own so you can enjoy the addictive crispy-fried parcels whenever you want. The dough rarely gets as good and thin as the ready-made stuff but it's still tasty.

MAKES ABOUT 30 DOUGH WRAPPERS

200ml/7fl oz/scant 1 cup water
250g/9oz/2 cups strong white bread flour
45g/1½oz/scant ½ cup cornflour

1. Bring the water to the boil and leave to cool slightly. Work the water and bread flour together in a bowl. The dough should be smooth and not sticky, so add more water or flour if needed to get a good consistency. The more the dough is worked, the shinier and more supple it will get. Knead for approximately 10 minutes.

2. Sprinkle the work surface with cornflour and roll the dough into a sausage shape about 2–3cm/¾–1¼in thick. Divide the dough into 30 equally sized pieces.

3. Roll the pieces into small balls. Roll the dough balls out with a rolling pin into thin round sheets, about 10cm/4in in diameter. Keep in a damp kitchen towel until ready to fill or freeze.

GYOZA WITH PRAWNS

Use fresh, raw prawns to make sure the filling sticks together in the dough. If you use cooked prawns the filling crumbles. If you can't get hold of red prawns you can always use the tails from fresh scampi.

MAKES 20

150g/5½oz frozen gyoza dough wrappers

4 tbsp vegetable oil

100g/3½oz white cabbage, finely chopped

4 spring onions, finely sliced

1 garlic clove, finely chopped

125ml/4fl oz/generous ½ cup water

200g/7oz raw red prawns or scampi, peeled

1½ tsp sesame oil

1 tbsp finely grated ginger root

2 tbsp finely chopped coriander

½ tsp salt

1 tsp cornflour

dipping sauces of your choice, see page 136
    and Sriracha sauce

1. Defrost the dough wrappers in the fridge overnight or leave at room temperature for a few hours.

2. Heat 2 tbsp of the vegetable oil in a frying pan and sauté the cabbage until it colours slightly. Add 2 of the spring onions and fry for a few minutes more.

3. Add the garlic and 3 tbsp of the water. Let the water absorb into the cabbage. Transfer the cabbage to a bowl and leave to cool.

4. Finely chop the prawns into a mince. Mix the cabbage with the sesame oil, ginger, coriander and salt.

5. Take approximately 1 tbsp of the mixture and place in the middle of a dough wrapper. Dip your finger in cold water and moisten the edges of the dough.

6. Fold the dough over the filling and squeeze, making sure no air is trapped. Make pleats so that the dough is shaped into a small parcel. Continue with the rest of the parcels.

7. Heat the remaining 2 tbsp oil in a frying pan. Place all the dough parcels closely together in the pan. Fry over a medium heat for a few minutes, until golden brown underneath.

8. Mix 5 tbsp water and the cornflour in a bowl. Pour over the gyoza. Cover with a lid or foil. Leave to steam for approximately 3 minutes. Lift the lid and let all the liquid steam away so that the starch from the cornflour turns into a crispy golden brown layer underneath the gyoza.

9. Turn the frying pan upside down over a plate. Sprinkle with the remaining spring onion. Serve warm with dipping sauces and Sriracha sauce.

GYOZA WITH MUSHROOM

Fry the mushrooms thoroughly in a hot pan so that they get a nice flavour. It will make a huge difference to the end result. And when you blend everything together into a coarse purée, think half blended, half in chunks for the right consistency.

MAKES 20

150g/5½ oz frozen gyoza dough wrappers

4 tbsp vegetable oil

250g/9oz mushrooms, e.g. shiitake or oyster, finely chopped

100g/3½oz white cabbage, finely chopped

4 spring onions, finely shredded

1 garlic clove, finely chopped

125ml/4fl oz/generous ½ cup water

1½ tsp sesame oil

1 tsp salt

1 tsp cornflour

dipping sauces of your choice, see page 136 and Sriracha sauce

1. Defrost the dough wrappers in the fridge overnight or leave at room temperature for a few hours.

2. Heat 2 tbsp of the oil in a frying pan and fry the mushrooms over a fairly high heat until they colour. Transfer to a bowl.

3. Heat the remaining 2 tbsp oil in the frying pan and sauté the cabbage until it colours slightly. Add 2 of the spring onions and fry for a few minutes. Add the garlic and 3 tbsp of the water. Leave to absorb into the cabbage.

4. Transfer the cabbage to the bowl with the mushrooms and leave to cool. Stir in the sesame oil and salt.

5. Blend into a coarse purée.

6. Take approximately 1 tbsp of the mixture and place in the middle of a dough wrapper. Dip your finger in cold water and moisten the edges of the dough.

7. Fold the dough over the filling and squeeze, making sure no air is trapped. Pleat the edges to form a small parcel. Continue with the rest of the parcels.

8. Place all the dough parcels closely together in the frying pan. Fry over a medium heat for a few minutes, until golden brown underneath.

9. Mix together the remaining water and the cornflour in a bowl. Pour over the gyoza. Cover with a lid or foil. Leave to steam for approximately 3 minutes. Lift the lid and let all the liquid steam away so that the starch from the cornflour turns into a crispy golden brown layer underneath the gyoza.

10. Turn the frying pan upside down over a plate. Sprinkle with the remaining spring onion. Serve warm with dipping sauces and Sriracha sauce.

GYOZA WITH PORK

The most classic filling for gyoza – pork mince and chopped cabbage with soy sauce, sesame, onion and ginger. The parcels get steamed on the top and lovely and crispy on the bottom.

MAKES 20

150g/5½oz frozen gyoza dough wrappers

4 tbsp vegetable oil

100g/3½oz white cabbage, finely chopped

4 spring onions, finely sliced

1 garlic clove, grated

125ml/4fl oz/generous ½ cup water

200g/7oz minced pork

1½ tsp sesame oil

1 tbsp finely grated ginger root

1 tsp salt

1 tsp cornflour

dipping sauces of your choice, see page 136 and Sriracha sauce

1. Defrost the dough wrappers in the fridge overnight or leave at room temperature for a few hours.

2. Heat 2 tbsp of the vegetable oil in a frying pan and sauté the cabbage until it colours slightly. Add 2 of the spring onions and fry for a few minutes more.

3. Add the garlic and 5 tbsp of the water. Let the water absorb into the cabbage. Transfer to a bowl and leave to cool.

4. Mix the cabbage with the minced pork, sesame oil, ginger and salt.

5. Take approximately 1 tbsp of the mixture and place in the middle of a dough wrapper. Dip your finger in cold water and moisten the edges of the dough.

6. Fold the dough over the filling and squeeze, making sure no air is trapped. Pleat the edges to form a small parcel. Continue with the rest of the parcels.

7. Mix together one or several dipping sauces.

8. Heat the remaining 2 tbsp oil in a frying pan. Place all the dough parcels closely together in the frying pan. Fry over a medium heat for a few minutes, until golden brown underneath.

9. Mix the cornflour and remaining water in a bowl. Pour over the gyoza. Cover with a lid or foil. Leave to steam for approximately 3 minutes. Lift the lid and let all the liquid steam away so that the starch from the cornflour turns into a crispy golden brown layer underneath the gyoza.

10. Turn the frying pan upside down over a plate. Sprinkle with the remaining spring onion. Serve warm with dipping sauces and preferably Sriracha sauce.

GYOZA DIPPING SAUCES

Half of the pleasure of eating gyoza is the actual dipping. The crispy fried parcel is dipped into a sauce that can be varied to infinity. The most classic is probably just soy sauce mixed with vinegar but there are lots of flavours that go together with the different fillings.

SALT & SOUR

   3 tbsp Japanese soy sauce

   3 tbsp rice vinegar

Mix the ingredients together in a bowl.

CHILLI & GINGER

   3 tbsp chilli oil, see page 29

   1 tbsp finely grated ginger

   1 tsp sesame oil

   3 tbsp Japanese soy sauce

   2 tbsp rice vinegar

Mix the ingredients together in a bowl.

SOY SAUCE & GARLIC

   3 tbsp Japanese soy sauce

   2 tbsp rice vinegar

   2 garlic cloves, finely chopped

   ½ tbsp toasted sesame seeds, crushed

   1 spring onion, finely shredded

Mix the ingredients together in a bowl.

SESAME & LEMON

   2 tbsp Japanese sesame paste (neri goma) or tahini

   3 tbsp water

   2 tbsp freshly squeezed lemon or yuzu juice

   1 tsp finely grated lemon zest or yuzu zest

   2 tbsp Japanese soy sauce

   1 tbsp toasted sesame seeds, crushed

Mix the ingredients together in a bowl.

PONZU

   1 piece of kombu seaweed (3–4g)

   3 tbsp Japanese soy sauce

   1½ tbsp sake (optional)

   1 tbsp mirin

   1 tbsp rice vinegar

   1½ tbsp lemon or yuzu juice

   finely grated zest of ½ lemon or ⅓ yuzu

1.   Place the kombu, soy sauce, sake and mirin in a pan and bring to the boil.

2.   Remove from the heat and leave to cool.

3.   Stir in the rice vinegar and lemon or yuzu juice and zest

MISO & SESAME PASTE

   2 tbsp water

   1 tbsp rice vinegar

   2 tbsp white miso

   2 tbsp fermented bean and chilli paste (tobanjan)

Mix the ingredients together in a bowl.

OKONOMIYAKI

THIS DISH IS PROOF THAT SOMETHING AS SIMPLE as cabbage can be lifted to great heights. The cabbage pancake, okonomiyaki, is served in all sorts of places, from underground stations to sushi joints and classic okonomiyaki restaurants with large griddles instead of tables.

The pancake is topped with a sweet soy-based sauce (not dissimilar to Worcestershire sauce), mayo, dried nori seaweed and thinly shaved bonito tuna. When the bonito flakes land on top of the hot pancake they move about in the steam – often called 'dancing bonito'. There are two different kinds of okonomiyaki: one that only contains cabbage and one that also contains noodles.

I usually like making everything from scratch when it comes to sauces and spice pastes, but here is the exception. If there is one ready-made ingredient that has been accepted by chefs around the world, it's the Japanese Kewpie mayonnaise. It's creamy and quite high in acidity – and nothing beats it on top of a sushi roll, in a bánh mì sandwich or on okonomiyaki. Strangely enough everyone turns a blind eye to the list of ingredients and happily gulps down big dollops of the mayonnaise from the kawaii-cute soft plastic bottle picturing a baby.

All countries have their traditions for using up leftovers. Okonomiyaki is the Japanese version. You can mix in whatever you've got in the fridge: cabbage, vegetables, mushrooms and meat. The important thing is to always have cabbage in the batter as it will make the pancake stick together in the pan, and without cabbage it's not a proper okonomiyaki. My favourite thing is to swap some of the cabbage for kimchi.

OKONOMIYAKI SAUCE

The mayonnaise and the sauce that go on the okonomiyaki are extremely important. There is a ready-made sauce available to buy in Japanese food stores, in a soft plastic bottle, similar to the Kewpie bottle. The sauce is like a mixture of Worcestershire sauce and teriyaki sauce. Here is a version that you can cook at home if you can't find the ready-made stuff.

SERVES 4–6

3 tbsp Worcestershire sauce

3 tbsp Japanese soy sauce

2 tbsp mirin

1 tbsp demerara sugar

1 tbsp rice vinegar

1½ tsp grated ginger

1 tsp cornflour

4 tbsp water

1. Add all the ingredients except the cornflour and 1 tbsp of the water to a pan and bring to the boil.

2. Whisk the cornflour with the reserved water and stir into the sauce. Bring to the boil so that the sauce thickens.

3. Leave to cool and store in the fridge.

OKONOMIYAKI OSAKA STYLE

The okonomiyaki from Osaka is the most famous one. It's without noodles and is fried like a thick pancake.

SERVES 4–6

500g/1lb 2oz white cabbage, chopped

4 spring onions, finely sliced

2½ tbsp finely chopped pickled ginger (gari)

2 tsp salt

250ml/9fl oz/generous 1 cup water

225g/8oz/heaped 1¾ cups plain flour

4 eggs

3 tbsp vegetable oil

140g/5oz bacon

6 tbsp okonomiyaki sauce, see page 139,
    or shop bought

6 tbsp mayonnaise, preferably Kewpie

2 tsp dried, crumbled nori seaweed

4 tbsp bonito flakes (katsuobushi)

1. Mix the cabbage, spring onion, ginger and salt together in a bowl.

2. In a separate bowl, whisk together the water, flour and eggs.

3. Mix the batter with the cabbage mixture.

4. Heat half the oil in a small frying pan (approximately 16–18cm/6–7in in diameter).

5. Pour half of the batter into the pan and shape into a flat pancake using a large spatula.

6. Lower the heat to medium and cover with a lid or aluminium foil. Leave to fry covered with a lid for approximately 10 minutes.

7. Cover the pancake with half of the bacon after 5 minutes. It should steam and the fat should seep into the cabbage.

8. Flip over with a large spatula – sometimes it's easier if you use two, to make sure the bacon stays in place. Fry covered with a lid or aluminium foil for approximately 5 minutes, until the pancake has coloured and the bacon is crispy.

9. Turn out the pancake upside-down on a plate so that the bacon is on the top.

10. Fry the second pancake. Keep the first pancake warm in the oven if needed, or eat it straight away. An okonomiyaki should preferably be eaten piping hot.

11. Drizzle with okonomiyaki sauce and mayonnaise. Sprinkle over the crumbled nori seaweed and bonito flakes.

~~~~~~~~~~~~~~~~~~~~

OKONOMIYAKI VARIATIONS

Kimchi okonomiyaki Swap half of the cabbage for kimchi.

Sauerkraut okonomiyaki Swap half of the cabbage for sauerkraut.

Veggie okonomiyaki Swap the bacon for chopped fresh shiitake mushrooms.

Swap the bacon for fried pork mince and mix it in with the batter.

Swap the bacon for boiled chicken (from chicken broth, see page 25) and mix it in with the batter.

Swap the bacon for boiled oxtail (from beef bone broth, see page 26) and mix it in with the batter.

OKONOMIYAKI HIROSHIMA STYLE

This version is perhaps more like an omelette packed with noodles and cabbage.

SERVES 2–4

1 portion ramen noodles, see page 38

110g/3¾oz/heaped ¾ cup plain flour

200ml/7fl oz/scant 1 cup water

1 tsp salt

2 tbsp mirin

3 tbsp vegetable oil

250g/9oz white cabbage, chopped

3 spring onions, finely sliced

140g/5oz bacon

3 tbsp Japanese soy sauce

2 tsp sesame oil

1 tbsp finely grated ginger

3 eggs

6 tbsp okonomiyaki sauce, see page 139,
    or shop bought

6 tbsp mayonnaise, preferably Kewpie

2 tsp dried, crumbled nori seaweed

4 tbsp bonito flakes (katsuobushi)

1. Boil the noodles for approximately 45 seconds in a pan of water on a rolling boil. It's best to use a noodle basket or a sieve so that you can quickly take out the noodles once done. You only have a window of a few seconds to make sure they're not under- or overcooked. Rinse the noodles in ice-cold water and shake off the excess water.

2. Whisk the flour, water, salt and mirin together to make a batter.

3. Heat 2 tbsp of the vegetable oil in a frying pan (approximately 30–40cm/12–16in in diameter). Pour half of the batter into the pan and top with the cabbage, spring onion and bacon slices. Fry for approximately 5 minutes over a medium heat.

4. Place a plate over the frying pan and turn the pancake upside down. Transfer to the pan again and fry the other side so that the bacon gets nice and crispy. Transfer to a plate and set aside.

5. Mix the noodles with the soy sauce, sesame oil and ginger.

6. Quickly whisk the eggs together.

7. Heat the remaining 1 tbsp oil in the frying pan and pour in half of the eggs. Top with the noodles and pour over the rest of the eggs. Tip in the fried cabbage pancake so that the cabbage faces downwards against the batter in the pan.

8. Fry over a low heat for approximately 10 minutes, until the batter has set.

9. Turn upside down. You will have a layer each of egg, noodles and cabbage pancake.

10. Serve topped with okonomiyaki sauce, mayonnaise, nori seaweed and bonito flakes.

Chilli pickled cucumber, pickled pink ginger, pickled apricots, pickled aubergine, soy pickled shiitake and pickled ginger.

TSUKEMONO

PICKLED APRICOTS – UMEBOSHI

Tsukemono are pickled vegetables with salty, sweet and sour flavours. Pickled plums are a classic tsukemono. The small Japanese plums, ume, are more similar to apricots so when you prepare this at home it's fine to use dried apricots that have been salted and added to a sour brine. This is a simplified recipe since umeboshi otherwise takes a few days to make.

MAKES ABOUT 1 LITRE/35FL OZ

> 700ml/24fl oz/3 cups water
>
> 2 tbsp sea salt
>
> 250g/9oz dried apricots
>
> 300ml/10½fl oz/1¼ cups rice vinegar
>
> 75g/2½oz/heaped ⅓ cup granulated sugar

1. Bring 500ml/17fl oz/generous 2 cups of the water to the boil with the salt. Add the apricots and simmer for approximately 10 minutes. Drain.

2. In a separate pan, bring the vinegar and sugar to the boil with the remaining water to make the brine. Mix with the apricots and transfer to a thoroughly cleaned jar with a tight-fitting lid. Close the lid and leave to cool. Unopened it keeps for up to 6 months in the fridge.

PICKLED GINGER – GARI

No ready-made pickled ginger beats home pickled. It's nice to serve as a side to ramen, gyoza, okonomiyaki and sushi, and also shredded as a topping for ramen. Often you get pickled ginger that is bright pink. It is either coloured with some kind of food colouring or you're lucky and it's coloured the classic way with red shiso. I sometimes make a version with beetroot: bring the brine to the boil together with a grated beetroot, strain and pickle the ginger in the pink brine.

MAKES APPROXIMATELY 400ML/ 14FL OZ/1⅔ CUPS

> 250ml/9fl oz/generous 1 cup rice vinegar
>
> 75g/2½oz/heaped ⅓ cup granulated sugar
>
> 2 tsp salt
>
> 250g/9oz ginger root, peeled

1. Slice or shred the ginger.

2. In a pan, bring the vinegar, sugar and salt to the boil.

3. Mix together the brine and ginger in a jar with a tight-fitting lid and leave to stand in the fridge for at least 24 hours before serving. The ginger will keep in an unopened jar for up to 1 year.

SALT PICKLED CUCUMBER

If you use pickling cucumbers the pickles will become a little firmer and chewier than if you use a standard cucumber. They will usually keep for longer too.

MAKES APPROXIMATELY 200G/7OZ

 4 pickling cucumbers or 1 standard cucumber

 2 tsp salt

 60ml/2fl oz/¼ cup rice vinegar

 2 tbsp granulated sugar

 2 tsp toasted sesame seeds

1. Slice the cucumber into 5mm/¼in thick slices and place in a bowl with the salt. Leave for 30 minutes.
2. Bring vinegar and sugar to the boil. Leave to cool.
3. Strain the liquid from the cucumber.
4. Mix the cucumber, brine and sesame seeds in a jar with a tight-fitting lid. Leave in the fridge for 2–3 days before serving. Keeps for up to 2 weeks.

CHILLI PICKLED CUCUMBER

A quick tsukemono from fresh cucumber.

SERVES 4

 1 cucumber

 ½ tsp sea salt

 1 tbsp chilli oil, see page 29

 1 tbsp rice vinegar

1. Bash the cucumber into pieces. Mix with salt and refrigerate for 20 minutes. Add the oil and vinegar.

SOY PICKLED SHIITAKE

If you use shiitake and morels that are left over from making mushroom broth you can skip steps 1 and 2. You get a small batch of pickles and it's a perfect way to use up the mushrooms that have boiled in the broth.

MAKES APPROXIMATELY 2 LITRES/ 3 ½ PINTS/8 CUPS

 1 litre/1¾ pints/4⅓ cups dried shiitake

 1.5 litres/2½ pints/6½ cups boiling hot water

 250ml/9fl oz/generous 1 cup Japanese soy sauce

 250ml/9fl oz/generous 1 cup rice vinegar

 150g/5½oz/¾ cup granulated sugar

 2 star anise

 1 garlic clove, crushed

 10cm/4in ginger root, peeled and sliced

1. Place the dried mushrooms in a bowl and top with the boiling hot water.
2. Leave to stand for 30 minutes. Strain and save 400ml/14fl oz/1⅔ cups of the liquid.
3. Bring the liquid (or a similar quantity of water if you're using mushrooms from the broth) to the boil together with the soy sauce, vinegar, sugar, star anise, garlic and ginger.
4. Mix the mushrooms and the brine in jars with tight-fitting lids. Press down the mushrooms so that they are covered with liquid.
5. Leave to stand in the fridge for at least 1 week before serving. The mushrooms will keep for up to 3 months.

かおたんラーメン

高　湯　中国福建省の高級スープ。

In a small shack near Nishi Crossing
you will find the ramen place Kaotan
which attracts everyone from hungry
road workers in the daytime to drunk
businessmen in the middle of the night.

INDEX

First published in the United Kingdom in 2017 by
Pavilion
43 Great Ormond Street
London
WC1N 3HZ

© 2016 Tove Nilsson
Natur & Kultur, Stockholm

ISBN 978-1-91121-644-5

A CIP catalogue record for this book is available from the British Library.

10 9 8 7 6

Reproduction by Mission Productions Ltd, Hong Kong
Printed in China

www.pavilionbooks.com

Recipe photographs: Roland Persson
Location photographs and design: Jonas Cramby
Editor: Maria Nilsson

The publisher would like to thank Frida Green for her work on this book.

THANKS!

To the absolute best publisher, Natur & Kultur.

To my publisher and editor, Maria Nilsson, who's always up to date on food, drink and cookbooks.

To photographer Roland Persson, for fantastic food photography and because you always happily slurp up leftover broth and noodles.

To designer Jonas Cramby, because apart from creating a nice design, you have also travelled to Tokyo to eat ramen and take super-nice location photographs.

To Niklas because you cook me the tastiest ramen and always make me happy.

To friends and family who have eaten, tested and cooked the ramen dishes in this book.